Confluences 1

Essays on the New Canadian Literature

edited by
Nurjehan Aziz

MAWENZI
HOUSE

We acknowledge the support of the Canada Council for the Arts for our publishing program. We also acknowledge support from the Government of Ontario through the Ontario Arts Council.

ONTARIO ARTS COUNCIL
CONSEIL DES ARTS DE L'ONTARIO
an Ontario government agency
un organisme du gouvernement de l'Ontario

Canada Council for the Arts
Conseil des arts du Canada

Cover design by Angel Guerra

Library and Archives Canada Cataloguing in Publication

Confluences 1 : essays on the new Canadian literature / Nurjehan Aziz, editor.

Includes bibliographical references.
ISBN 978-1-927494-84-4 (paperback)

1. Canadian literature – 20th century – History and criticism. 2. Canadian literature – 21st century – History and criticism. I. Aziz, Nurjehan, editor

PS8117.C66 2016 C810.9'0054 C2016-907184-7

Printed and bound in Canada by Coach House Printing.

Mawenzi House Publishers Ltd.
39 Woburn Avenue (B)
Toronto, Ontario M5M 1K5
Canada
www.mawenzihouse.com

Contents

Preface

In the past four decades Canadian literature, reflecting the nation itself, has become increasingly diverse; poets and fiction writers of different backgrounds and sensibilities, inspired by various traditions, geographies, and histories continue to contribute to it in greater numbers, in this way expanding our imaginative spaces. Canadian literature is exciting. We at Mawenzi House have always believed that such literary works not be treated as transitory, their interest and relevance not be only of the moment. A literature grows when it is examined critically, and its multiple facets are exposed and discussed, and held up for greater discussion. In other words, a mature and growing literary criticism reflecting Canada's diversity is necessary. In this volume, which we expect to be the first of a series, we begin Mawenzi's contribution to this process.

NURJEHAN AZIZ

MICHAEL ONDAATJE

Fielding Ondaatje: A Brief Look at the "Canadian" Response

Aparna Halpé

In the Canadian literary environment of the late twentieth century, Michael Ondaatje's early work consistently spawned a heated critical debate over the poetics of cultural representation. Critical readings of the 1980s polarized Ondaatje's oeuvre along lines that define a projected split between the "West" (Canada) and an implied "East" (Sri Lanka). Following select critical reception of *Running in the Family* (1982) and the early poetry,[1] I argue that the trope of the nation provides a helpful point of entry into some of the key criticisms levelled at Ondaatje. The anxiety over Ondaatje's narration of Sri Lanka invites a particularly complex negotiation of issues of agency and location that, in turn, provokes a varied and fruitful exploration of differing critical practices. Likewise, the insistent call to dialogue between Canadian and Sri Lankan critics, sounded by diasporic scholars of South Asian origin, opens out a range of analytical strategies from the purely anecdotal to the intensely scholarly that intersect and interrogate each other in numerous ways. At root, however, I point out the tendency to project meaning onto Ondaatje's texts according to the particular biases and preoccupations of location and frames of discourse.[2]

I begin by focusing on two important early essays on Ondaatje by Linda Hutcheon and J Edward Chamberlin that appear in Solecki's collection *Spider Blues*. While Hutcheon and Chamberlin articulate entirely differing points of critical focus, they share a common concern with the way Ondaatje revolutionizes literary convention while remaining firmly fixed in the recognizable language of twentieth-century poetics. Hutcheon and Chamberlin also suggest that the "newness" of this approach demonstrates a negotiation of inheritance (literary and otherwise) that is somehow tied to Ondaatje's position as a diasporic writer in the Canadian literary landscape. The different focal points provided by these two early responses reflect the tendency to read Ondaatje within critical frames that primarily foreground his use of artifice and invention. These readings demonstrate the difficulty involved in interrogating the complex issue of Ondaatje's cultural belongings.

Solecki's comprehensive collection of essays is important because it outlines a distinctly Canadian response to Ondaatje's early work. Solecki's gathering of critics attempts to locate Ondaatje within an emergent understanding of a specifically Canadian literature. Significantly, Solecki's choice of critic also reflects the particularly "Canadian" focus of this project—of the nineteen scholars who contributed to this volume, only Ernest MacIntyre speaks with some authority on Ondaatje's literary heritage as a diasporic Sri Lankan writer, and MacIntyre is not Canadian. This is not to say that the Canadian critics ignore Ondaatje's Sri Lankan literary inheritances. For example, in the absence of a body of critical scholarship on Ondaatje's Sri Lankan influences, Chamberlin suggests a provocative reading of early poetry, including *The Dainty Monsters* (1967), *The Collected Works of Billy the Kid* (1970), *Rat Jelly* (1973) and *There's a Trick with a Knife I'm Learning to Do* (1979), that remains faithful to Ondaatje's own ambiguous construction of sociocultural inheritance. However, the more prevalent critical response to Ondaatje's Sri Lankan content involves a highly exoticized reading of Sri Lanka where Ondaatje's use of artifice is frequently mistaken for representation. This trend in Ondaatje scholarship was to change, as I argue below, with the arrival of South Asian critics in the inner circle of Canadian literary criticism.

The essays in *Spider Blues* deal largely with the difficulty of framing Ondaatje's experimental, genre-bending corpus in familiar literary terms. Ondaatje is read comparatively beside writers like Margaret Atwood, Rudy Wiebe or Robert Kroetsch, suggesting particular consonances in theme and approach that reinforce his position as a Canadian writer while foregrounding his own peculiar brand of literary postmodernism. Ondaatje's literary border-crossings are read as symptomatic of a negotiation of hybridity based on his varied literary and cultural inheritances. Hutcheon, for example, suggests that his particular melange of history, memoir, and fiction is best described as "historiographic metafiction" (302). Framing Ondaatje within a particular postmodernist discourse, Hutcheon goes on to claim that "poetry, fiction, biography, even history—all are texts and must be read as such, that is, with suspicion" (303). In Hutcheon's terms, reading with a sense of suspicion involves a process of deconstruction of "textual forces" that paradoxically demand a consequent reconstruction of meaning from the reader.

Foregrounding the readerly act of interpretation accomplishes several things for Hutcheon. Most importantly, it lends a particular authority to the reader who deconstructs the text purely in terms of literary content, ignoring, as it were, the nuanced and often troubled sociopolitical contexts that the author writes into his work. For example, writing on *Running*, Hutcheon claims that "it is even more clearly the reader, participating in the act of organizing the past, who constitutes the focus of this book" (304). This "act of organization" suggests that the reader has particular agency in the way the content of *Running* plays out on the historical stage. Hutcheon enacts just such an "organization" in her reading of Ondaatje's Sri Lanka: "Ceylon, conveniently, has a city called Colombo, but even without it, Ondaatje's island bears many resemblances to García Márquez's Columbian Macondo: the extreme of heat, drought, and flood; the exuberant vegetation; the incessant insect activity; the almost mythically exaggerated inhabitants . . . " (308). The act of reading "Ceylon" via the Columbian Macondo (a parallel pulled out of the homophonic similarity between Sri Lanka's commercial capital, Colombo, and García Márquez's fictionalized Columbia) leads to the most unfortunate exotification of Ondaatje's subject matter. This reading of Ondaatje's literary mongrelism depends entirely on fixing the content of *Running* as a particular form of artifice that is, in turn, deconstructed via Hutcheon's individual perception of literary tradition—a reading that is unfortunately wide of the mark. In the race to claim Ondaatje as a Canadian postmodernist writer, Hutcheon chooses to remain ignorant of the specifics of Ondaatje's texts, particularly those that involve a Sri

Lankan content.[3]

It is the issue of tradition that proves most complex in the early readings of Ondaatje. Chamberlin correctly demonstrates that in relation to Ondaatje, the very notion of tradition involves an internal contradiction: " . . . there is another set of contradictions less easy to delineate, contradictions that involve a sense of what we sometimes refer to as a poet's traditions, by which we usually mean inheritances that somehow are less powerful than conventions and yet more binding than obligations" (31). Chamberlin unpacks this notion of tradition and inheritance carefully, suggesting that for Ondaatje, tradition is not an issue of language, but of form. Chamberlin is one of the first critics to point out that Ondaatje's use of language is entirely conventional at a time when postcolonial authors like Derek Walcott or Seamus Heaney were reworking their consonant forms of Englishes (35). Chamberlin suggests that "contradiction" inhabits the gap between literary traditions and cultural inheritances. In his reading, Ondaatje's bizarre experiments in form hint at his negotiation of many literary traditions which are, sometimes, contradictory: "The difficulty is in recognizing these contradictions, for although they bedevil and inspire those contemporary poets who have a heightened sense of the distance between their literary and their cultural inheritances, they are hidden behind our superficial understanding of the idea of tradition" (31). Like Hutcheon, this reading places the onus of criticism on the reader. However, Chamberlin also demands that this reader be thoroughly informed about the rules of Ondaatje's game. Chamberlin recognizes an aesthetic of contradiction in the early poems and links it to Ondaatje's shape-shifting essays in literary convention. In Chamberlin's words, "Ondaatje is engaged in a process of trying to purify not the dialect of the tribe—that was presumably done by the modernists—but the ways in which the author and the reader reach agreement that what is said is, to use conventional terminology, beautiful and true" (35).

For the Canadian postcolonial critic, this sense of agreement proves notoriously difficult. Chamberlin concludes his essay with this curious statement: "Canada offers Ondaatje a geography, but no inheritance; Sri Lanka offers him a family history, but no tradition, no way of passing things on; the English language offers him both an inheritance and a history, but no time and place" (41). The suggestion that Sri Lanka offers Ondaatje a "family history, but no tradition" is unusual in the context of *Running*. If we follow Chamberlin's reading of tradition as the congruence of literary and sociocultural inheritances, then we are bound to recognize that the narrator of *Running* speaks out of the voices of his inheritances. These can be personal, as in the voice of his mother, Doris (86), or drawn from cultural echoes like the voice of the dead poet Lakdasa Wikkramasinha (68). This is a borrowed language, and its peculiar intonation and articulation is certainly passed on. This language, Ondaatje's English, is bound to the many times and places he carries within himself as a diasporic writer partly educated in Sri Lanka, England, and Canada. It is shaped by the more contemporary inheritance of writing in Canada during a literary renaissance peopled by writers and poets such as bp nichol, Rudy Wiebe, Margaret Atwood, and Robert Kroetsch. Chamberlin's assertion is not so much about Ondaatje but about the difficulty that the early critics encountered in hearing Ondaatje's multiple linguistic inheritances, a difficulty that contemporaneous Sri Lankan critics faced in a very different way.

Both Hutcheon and Chamberlin respond to Ondaatje as a Canadian writer, his diasporic sensibilities being part of the familiar make up of an emergent multicultural Canadian literature. We do not see any attempt in their criticism to engage in a dialogue with other critics writing from Ondaatje's erstwhile homelands. To be fair, Ondaatje's writing doesn't immediately demand such a cross-cultural critical dialogue. However, by the mid 80s, critics of South Asian heritage—among them Arun Mukherjee, Chelva Kanaganayakam, and Suwanda Sugunasiri—were to write against this Canadianist approach, calling for a greater engagement with the work offered by Sri Lankan scholars. In her essay "The Sri Lankan Poets in Canada: An Alternative View," Arun Mukherjee draws on a major Sri Lankan critic like Yasmine Gooneratne and an emerging voice like Qadri Ismail to reinforce her own reading of Ondaatje. Pointing out the prevalent tendency to read Ondaatje outside sociopolitical frames, Mukherjee cites the critical response from Sri Lanka as sharply revisionist in ways that foreground issues of context over poetics. Mukherjee asks, "Would it not be worthwhile for them [the

Canadian critics] to find out what Sri Lankans might have to say about Ondaatje's work?" (Mukherjee 74). "Lefting" the balance, Mukherjee quotes from an early student essay by Qadri Ismail that uses Edward Said's theory of Orientalism as a frame for reading Ondaatje. Ismail complains that Ondaatje "tells us nothing of the colonial experience—or of himself" (Mukherjee 74), an objection raised more in reference to Ondaatje's mode of narration than to an actual absence of colonial experience (73-74). Ismail claims that Ondaatje's poems are "beautifully written—and insipid" (74), a critique echoed by Mukherjee, who finds her own critical positions reinforced by Ismail.[4] Curiously, both Ismail and Mukherjee concentrate on Ondaatje's use of artifice and his adherence to literary convention as a cause for contention. It is Ondaatje's unwillingness to ascribe overt "meaning" beyond the poetics of narration that fuels Mukherjee and Ismail's critique of a lack of sociopolitical engagement. This is, of course, tantamount to a U-turn from the positions taken by Hutcheon and Chamberlin.

Mukherjee's call to include Sri Lankan critics in the Canadian response to Ondaatje was realized in the Spring volume of *Canadian Literature* (1992). This issue is dedicated to Ondaatje's work, and for the first time includes two important essays by Canadian critics of Sri Lankan origin—Chelva Kanaganayakam and Suwanda Sugunasiri. Sugunasiri's essay attempts to provide a sociopolitical and historical frame for Ondaatje's work and, at the same time, offers a critique of Mukherjee's reading of "Lankanness." Kanaganayakam provides a thorough engagement with the issue of literary convention and Ondaatje's diasporic sensibility, and addresses the claims made by major critics like Hutcheon. Both critics explore the implications of reading Ondaatje's figurative visions of "Ceylon" as representative of postcolonial Sri Lanka. While both scrutinize the way Ondaatje narrativizes Sri Lanka, Sugunasiri, in particular, reads historical bias into Ondaatje's writing, through a set of assumptions based on the critic's own "personal experience" (63) of midtwentieth-century Sri Lanka.

Sugunasiri takes Mukherjee to task for misreading Ondaatje through a predominantly "Indian" lens: "It is simply that she [Mukherjee] has, because of an understandable unfamiliarity with Sri Lankan society, generalized and extended from her own Indian society, fallen into the trap of being ahistorical and acontextual, crimes she pins on Ondaatje" (64). Sugunasiri provides no concrete evidence that substantiates this charge, but his observation alerts us to the varying degrees of conflict that arise when critics attempt to read Ondaatje's response to "history" in the Sri Lankan context. Sugunasiri implies that Mukherjee's reading is both ahistorical and acontextual but does not seem to be conscious of the lack of balanced context in his professed "personal" sociohistorical reading of pre-Independence Sri Lanka: "While this rough profile [of pre-Independence Sri Lanka], based on personal experience, should not pass for a rigorous sociological analysis, it does provide us with a broad, and I believe, an authentic picture of pre-1956 society" (63). Sugunasiri's construction of twentieth-century Sri Lankan class structure falls particularly hard on the Burghers, the people of mixed descent to whom Ondaatje "belongs" racially and culturally.[5] When Sugunasiri claims that Ondaatje "*was* (through his community and class) the colonizer!" (64), he puts forward a monolithic reading of the Burghers as "Eurasian sub-stratum elite" (63) that ignores their wide-ranging status within the middle, lower-middle class and proletariat in colonial and postcolonial Sri Lanka. When Sugunasiri claims that Ondaatje and fellow Canadian poet Rienzi Crusz (also Burgher) are the "bourgeoisie that fled the revolution" (67), he offers no contextual reading of the systematic alienation of the Burghers by the Sinhala-only policies of 1956 that led to the first major exodus of Burghers and Tamils from the country.[6]

Sugunasiri's article demonstrates a particular anxiety of ownership over the Sri Lankan content of Ondaatje's work that extends into a sociohistorical analysis of the author himself. The issue of cultural representation becomes a battleground where Ondaatje is expected to stand witness to a particular vision of Sri Lankan-ness. Claiming the familiar adage that the "personal is political" (63), Sugunasiri offers a reading of *Running* through Ondaatje's personal history. However, at no point in the essay does Sugunasiri actually demonstrate a detailed familiarity with Ondaatje's so-called history beyond the fact that he was a Burgher, born in Ceylon during the time immediately preceding Independence. Furthermore, asserting that the Burghers are the elite of Sri Lanka (a troubling monolithic reading of an extremely heterogeneous group of people), Sugunasiri claims that Ondaatje, by token of his birth, "shared the Eurasian community psyche, remote from ideology and indeed from social reality" (63). Quite apart from the intensely problematic suggestion that all Burghers are somehow incapable of grasping social reality, this sentence demonstrates the complete lack of any evidence that actually locates Ondaatje within a specific "personal" or "political" context in the Ceylon of the mid 1950s. Sugunasiri goes on to suggest that Ondaatje cannot be accused of not representing the migrant Sri Lankan experience in Canada because "he experienced *no* displacement" (64).[7] The underlying assumption here is that by token of his racial background Ondaatje is already desensitized to any essential sense of Sri Lankan identity, a fact which makes him "essentially" Canadian.

Sugunasiri's reading of Ondaatje is an almost unconscious, visceral disavowal of Ondaatje's Sri Lankan heritage. In Sugunasiri's analysis, Ondaatje cannot bear witness to his Sri Lankan past because his privileged position within Lankan society precludes the ability to narrate the specificities of Lankan experience. Likewise, Mukherjee's reading of Ondaatje (which is a critique of Canadianist reading practices) suggests that Ondaatje's overt use of artifice leads to an exotification of the local. Let us momentarily place these critiques of Ondaatje beside Chamberlin when he says:

Chamberlin reminds us that Ondaatje's "particular time and place" is contemporary Canada. Likewise, as a diasporic, Ondaatje's articulation of time and place contains a resonating memory that speaks through all his many heritages. In Chamberlin's reading, heritage is not simply determined by birth or inheritance, it is edgy and tricksterish, shifting shape according to the contingencies of telling stories. As Chamberlin points out, Ondaatje's narrative acts of witness are built to invoke suspicion in the reader. The Ondaatjean speaker is most persuasive when he wears the most figurative of masks. In Chamberlin's words, "He is most himself when he is Philoctetes, say, and when Philoctetes is a spider" (38). We see that Chamberlin does not attempt to read Ondaatje through his narrator in the same way Sugunasiri does. Chamberlin recognizes the poet's position as witness, but also suggests that the act of bearing witness in narrative involves figurative leaps that are only partial, porous glimpses into history.

Mukherjee and Sugunasiri's critiques of Ondaatje reveal particular anxieties about the articulation of "originary" identities within a Canadian literary frame of reference. In this case, Ondaatje's depiction of Sri Lanka and Sri Lankan identities are deemed misrepresentations due to their failure to live up to critical expectations that prefabricate these categories. In Mukherjee's case, Ondaatje fails because his Ceylon is exoticized in the highest degree (73). For Sugunasiri, Ondaatje fails because his is not, essentially, a legitimate Sri Lankan voice. In both readings, Ondaatje's Canadianness is glossed over in search of a submerged Lankan racial and cultural identity. Furthermore, the issue of dislocation, fragmented cultural inheritance, and literary tradition is read through the critic's particular vision of how a Sri Lankan immigrant should respond to displacement.[8] Sugunasiri and Mukherjee also refuse to explore the issue of Ondaatje's literary tradition in any real depth. Although Mukherjee attempts to redress this issue by quoting "Sri Lankan" critics like Ismail,[9] she fails to engage directly with Ondaatje's sources—Robert Knox's *An Historical Relation* (1681), Lakdasa Wikkramasinha's poetry, the fifth-century rock graffiti at Sigiriya, or the more contemporary graffiti by students of the Vidyalankara campus incarcerated in 1971 on suspicion of insurgency. Mukherjee is content to take Ismail or Gooneratne's word on Sri Lankan Anglophone writing as authoritative, because she appears to believe that trusting the local critic is responsible critical practice.[10] Mukherjee's dependence on critiques offered by Sri Lankan scholars alerts us to the effort that the self-conscious postcolonial critic exerts when reading an author like Ondaatje. However, it is also significant that despite best intentions, these methods of literary analysis can fail because they read issues of representation through particular political and national biases. Because both Mukherjee and Sugunasiri focus explicitly on the issue of cultural representation, they seem unconcerned with the architectonics of Ondaatje's writing. As a result, they fail to connect the dots between Ondaatje's use of allusion and artifice, and his own distinctive mode of narrating Sri Lanka.

While the critical relation between artifice and representation still remains an issue, we see that in the hands of an astute reader like Kanaganayakam, the gaps and absences in Ondaatje's work offer a point of entry into the issue of framing Sri Lanka through multiple narrative traditions. Kanaganayakam's reading of *Running* is meticulously sourced, creating a cross-cultural dialogue between a range of scholarly material from Sri Lanka, Canada and elsewhere. Kanaganayakam is able to negotiate the issues of Ondaatje's race and class in relation to other writers of similar origin like Ernest MacIntyre and Jean Arasanayagam, some of the most important voices of late twentieth-century fiction, drama and poetry in Sri Lanka. Differentiating between the many factors that led to the migration of the Burghers from Sri Lanka, Kanaganayakam explores specific issues of diaspora and exile that make Ondaatje's concerns different in degree from a diasporic writer like MacIntyre: "Ondaatje left early enough to avoid the gradual disillusionment that set in among the Burghers in the latter part of the 1950s and early 1960s following the introduction of Sinhala as the official language and the switch to Sinhala and Tamil as the languages of instruction" (35). Clearly, Ondaatje is not an exile like MacIntyre, who lives through the "large-scale exodus from Sri Lanka to Melbourne" (35). However, Kanaganayakam demonstrates that the trauma of displacement isn't exclusively found within narratives of exile. Kanaganayakam's grasp of the relation between race, class, and migration suggests that despite all accusations of privilege, the experience of displacement, as narrated in *Running*, is real enough: " . . . the need to return finds expression through dreams that encroach into his [Ondaatje's] consciousness and through the marginal positions of sleeping on a couch at a friend's home" (35).

Kanaganayakam does not rest his assertions purely on reading Ondaatje's constructions of "self" as representational. The strength of his analysis lies in recognizing the fictionalization of the author's portrait of displacement. Kanaganayakam draws out subtle intertextual allusions in *Running* that echo canonical writers like Shakespeare and Austen as well as lesser known Sri Lankan poets like Wikkramasinha. His analysis of *Running* demonstrates that reading "history" in Ondaatje's work requires a thorough understanding of the full range of his literary inheritances. For example, the observation that Ondaatje's experimentation with genre is also linked to his particular negotiations of hybridity (which we encountered in the early criticism of Hutcheon, Chamberlin, Solecki, et al) takes on a new significance when Kanaganayakam reads the issue of alienation and displacement in *Running* through Ondaatje's allusion to Eliot:

> The sense of inadequacy, the anguish of having been severed from history comes across in a wonderful statement that intertextually recalls Prufrock; the author comments:
>
> After the cups of tea, coffee, public conversations . . . I want to sit down with someone and talk with utter directness, want to talk to all the lost history like that deserving lover. (54)
>
> The combination of urgency and self-consciousness is central to the work, for it defines the elusive tone of the book, points to the difficulty of attaching labels—"travelogue," "autobiography," "fiction"—all of which seem to be both true and false. (37)

Kanaganayakam's intertextual engagement alerts us to the fact that Ondaatje's written "quest of self" in *Running* also contains a highly sophisticated adaptation of the search for "originary" narrative that was so characteristic of the high modernists. As we see, Kanaganayakam's interstitial readings of literary inheritance and cultural representation afford a far greater range of critical complexity than we have encountered in previous attempts by Ondaatje's South Asian critics.

However, ultimately Kanaganayakam agrees with Mukherjee that Ondaatje's apolitical stance can smack of solipsism (36). Describing Ondaatje's depictions of insurgency during the 1970s, he concludes that the anecdote of young Sinhala insurgents playing cricket at the family grounds at Kegalle is ironic, and, therefore, "hardly amusing or convincing" (37). I would suggest that an alternate reading of this instance of irony would reveal that the passage is meant to be neither amusing nor convincing. Ondaatje's fateful juxtaposition of insurgents playing cricket is convincing only at the figurative level because it foregrounds a central issue in *Running*: the tragedy of youth in the victims of the 1971 insurrection. Kanaganayakam is careful not to suggest that Ondaatje's recalibrations of history are inauthentic (as Mukherjee and Sugunasiri claim), but he does conclude that the weakness of *Running* remains its "refusal to participate actively in the referential" (40). Thus, we arrive once more at the issue of representation. In Kanaganayakam's reading of Ondaatje, fractured representation is part and parcel of the narrative of displacement: "in foregrounding the 'narrative' at the expense of the 'national', Ondaatje abandons a wonderful opportunity to assert a much-needed sense of belonging" (41). Kanaganayakam suggests that the absence of an emotionally weighted position in relation to the trauma of recent Sri Lankan history precludes Ondaatje's capacity to belong to the island nation as a returned prodigal. Curiously, Kanaganayakam goes on to suggest that this failure is symptomatic: "In his failure, Ondaatje shares the shortcomings of the majority of Sri Lankan writing in English which, for the most part, has stayed clear of the upheavals that have transformed a kindly, generous nation into a cruel and mindless battlefield" (41). If Ondaatje's silence mirrors the silence of other Sri Lankan writers, then "silence" as a narrative act has marked him within a particular circle of belonging—that of the educated middle-class Anglophone writer who uses silence as a strategy that articulates trauma and the guilt of social immunity from present horrors.[11] The issue lies in the way we read "silence" as complacence or lack of commitment, when it can be the sign of trauma and guilt.

We see therefore, that Mukherjee, Sugunasiri, and Kanaganayakam read Ondaatje's refusal to adopt a defined position on the sociopolitical climate of Sri Lanka as a particular form of apathy, or a lack of engagement with the realities of nation-building. Sugunasiri claims that Ondaatje cannot respond to the idea of nation because he is representative of the colonizer—a problematic reading of race, class, and politics. Mukherjee, following Gooneratne and Ismail, suggests that Ondaatje "does not get drawn into the acts of living" (34). She defines "living" in a post-Independence Sri Lanka according to a particular political frame based on a primarily Marxist and feminist theoretical position. When Kanaganayakam claims that Ondaatje foregrounds "narrative" at the expense of the "national" (40) he too calls for a kind of authorial consciousness that demonstrates a commitment to narrating the nation through a particular sociocultural engagement. I would suggest that if we turn the lens of scrutiny back on Mukherjee, Sugunasiri, and Kanaganayakam, we see that their preoccupation with narrating the "realities" of the emergent nation also reflects an anxiety over narrating Sri Lanka as the colonized "other" to postcolonial Canada. Although it is doubtful that Ondaatje intends to sell an exotic Kegalle to an enraptured Canadian audience, responses like Hutcheon's remind us that unfamiliarity is a space that can invite the most arbitrary inventions from both reader and critic. Mukherjee and Sugunasiri attempt to revise this ahistorical method of reading Ondaatje, but in doing so, they reflect their own particular concerns about the tension between diasporic and local modes of cultural representation. Conscious though he is that cultural representation in fiction is linked to the power of authority that a writer wields, and this power is inescapably tied to location, Kanaganayakam, in contradistinction to Mukherjee and Sugunasiri, is careful to address the difficulty that hyphenated critics face when tasked with the burden of negotiating the cultural slippages of hyphenated writers, who arguably wield more power on the reading public. Kanaganayakam's cultural and literary recalibrations deconstruct the naïve image of the diasporic writer as "originary" cultural ambassador even as they remind us of the power of representation inherent in fictional constructions of history.

Focusing in the main on the critical reception of *Running in the Family* and the early poetry, this article outlines the difficulty critics encounter when reading Ondaatje, whether they are Sri Lankan or Canadian, or both. We may read Ondaatje as Canadian, Sri Lankan, transnational, diasporic, and liberal humanist. We may accuse him for being too much or not enough of any of these things. But, quite often, our willingness to probe and dissect the vicissitudes of a postcolonial, postmodernist writer like Ondaatje are not complemented by a like-minded interrogation of our own critical biases and the influences of location, history, and story on our own analytical practices. When Kanaganayakam draws attention to the overtly celebratory approach fostered by the "Canadian" literary establishment, he also points out that such readings are contingent on issues of accessibility in a global literary environment. His important recalibrations offered by foreground the need for an articulate sociopolitical consciousness that scrutinizes the dynamics of power and privilege in diasporic narratives. In the early response to Ondaatje's writing, (with the single exception of Mukherjee's use of Ismail's early essay), there is a singular absence of material from the many literary critics living and working in Sri Lanka, such as Thiru Kandiah, Ashley Halpé, and DCRA Goonetilleke. These critics remain the silent third voice to the polarized discourse on belonging that we encounter in Ondaatje's Canadian critics. We see therefore, that in the vast body of critical literature surrounding Ondaatje's work, the projected conversation between international, diasporic, and local critic had not yet begun.[12] Canadianist Nick Mount asks whether Canadian critics have, as yet, learned to hear Canadian writers in their multivocality ("The Canlit Boom of the 1960s.") Extending this question to Ondaatje's Canadian, Sri Lankan, and Sri Lankan Canadian critics, I hazard to answer that we have only learned to hear him partially, at best.

This is an updated and revised version of "Fielding Ondaatje: A Brief Look at the 'Canadian' Response'," previously published in Moving Worlds: A Journal of Transcultural Writings, *edited by Shirley Chew and Chandani Lokuge, University of Leeds, School of English, 2010.*

MARLENE NOURBESE PHILIP

Caliban's Voice: Marlene Nourbese Philip's Poetic Response to Western Hegemonic Discourse

H Nigel Thomas

Marlene Nourbese Philip is one of several African Canadian poets whose work is devoted almost exclusively to the exploration of what constitutes an African Occidental identity. Some of these poets, George Elliot Clarke[1] and Maxine Tynes, for example, are descended from the Black Loyalists; others, like Claire Harris, Dionne Brand, Clifton Joseph, Lilian Allen, Horace Goddard, and Philip herself are immigrants to Canada from the Caribbean. Their poetry reflects an uneasiness with the space Africans of the diaspora occupy in language, in history, in myth, in economics—in short, in Western ontology.

If I may employ a figure elaborated by several scholar-writers, including George Lamming, Kofi Awoonor, and Max Dorsinville,[2] these poets confront in varying degrees and with varying intensity the Prospero component of Occidental reality as well as the African diaspora's response to that reality. Many of George Elliot Clarke's poems depict an African Nova Scotian culture that distinguishes itself from its European counterpart in ways analogous to those Edward Brathwaite outlines for folk Jamaican culture (Clarke 1983; Brathwaite 1981). The dub poets of Toronto, whose best-known representatives are Allen and Joseph, offer unlettered Black Torontonians a perspective apart from profit and consumption. Their performances foster community consolidation in ways reminiscent of the African American folk church and of African American poetry readings during the late Sixties and early Seventies

(Baker 1980, 128-29, Thomas 1988, 12-20).

Now to my subject. In "Journal Entries Against Racism," in her collection of essays *Frontiers* (Philip 1992), an entry made while Philip was composing the poems that comprise *She Tries Her Tongue: Her Silence Softly Breaks* (1989), reads thus:

> The white male thinks, and therefore is. He seldom, if ever, says or needs to say, I am; I am white; I am male; I am human. Everything around him conspires to transform mere attributes into qualities of apparent permanence and universality, synonymous with privilege. We might say these arguments are hackneyed and old hat. . . . But these issues crash in against the writing which is rooted in the word—"the 'paternal Word' sustained by a fight to the death between the two races (men/women)." Not to mention the father tongues imposed on us, the colonized peoples of colour. How to use the "paternal Word" to issue forth first statements—of wholeness? (Philip 1992, 67)

Herein lies Caliban's challenge: to make his word break through the surface of Prospero's propaganda. It reminds us of Du Bois's observation of the double-consciousness with which every African American must negotiate his or her reality (214-215) and presents us with the insuperable dilemma writers born and raised in colonies must confront inasmuch as the languages they employ are replete with metaphors that demean their ontology. Mikhail Bakhtin tells us that

> the artist receives no word in linguistically virginal form. The word is already impregnated by the practical situations and poetic contexts in which [she/] he has encountered it. . . . The work of the poet . . . can only effect a few transvaluations, a few displacements in intonations that the poet and his audience perceive against a background of previous evaluations and previous intonations. (Todorov 48-49)

Philip is aware, more so than Bakhtin perhaps, of this process: "We are all," she writes, "engaged in some form of dialogue with history, with literature, with the past, the present—even the future—expanding, clarifying, or modifying what someone else has already said, or trying to say it in some new way" (1992, 64). If we assume that Bakhtin speaks for artists integrated with their society, imagine how dire is the plight of those artists whose identity has been consigned to the shadow reality of their societies.

The entire collection of poems in *She Tries Her Tongue: Her Silence Softly Breaks* (1989) is about finding one's tongue. By the time readers get to the title poem (on page 84 of the Ragweed edition) they would have (1) read the introductory essay, which sensitizes them to the repressive role language played in the African diaspora; (2) experienced something of the destabilization and the obsessive but futile search for reunification engaged in by mother and child severed from each other, metaphors undoubtedly of the ontological reality of the African diaspora; (3) eavesdropped on an adult woman reflecting on the double-consciousness of her coming of age rituals; (4) witnessed the narrator's reflection, rendered sometimes in a stutter, on how the language proffered as a mother tongue had all the while been transmogrifying her; (5) listened to the narrator's reflections on the implications of a mother tongue that traumatizes, that is "a foreign anguish"; (6) seen the narrator fight back—in essence, watched her create a tongue and break her silence. Therefore, by the time that we get to the title poem, we have observed the narrator undoing Prospero's spells, rejecting his rituals, filling his space in her life with her own, employing a counter conjure barbed with the narrator's own curses.

Obviously there is insufficient space here to analyze all of these preoccupations and so I shall focus on the removal of spells. For this reason I shall examine two of the key poems in the text: (1) "Discourse on the Logic of Language," which examines the functions of a mother tongue, and (2) "Universal Grammar," which begins putting into place the elements for regenerating a "mothering" tongue. As mentioned above, there is great insistence on what must be uprooted, but there is less clarity about what would take its place. What is clear by the time we complete the poem "Universal Grammar" is that the colonizer/oppressor has been relegated to the status of a linguistic shadow. By then English words have been invested with connotations never ascribed to them by the dominant, oppressive culture, for whom language is a vehicle of self-exaltation. The blond beast, for example, known by Jung (107) and possibly a handful of whites, who, with erect penis, maxim guns, helicopter gunships, and lies, ready to waste for profit, power, and pleasure, is boldly shown to constitute the nightmare images of the sleeping and waking lives of the world's nonwhite populations.

Two distinct approaches of Philip's method of counter-conjure,[3] a method intended to deconstruct meanings reified by the dominant culture, are exemplified respectively in the poems "Discourse on the Logic of Language" and "Universal Grammar." In the case of the first poem, there are five separate discourses, each of which complements and enlarges the perspective for understanding that part of the poem we formally identify as poetry. In "Discourse on the Logic of Language," the reader recognizes in the centre column of the page words arranged in standard stanzaic poetic form, and proceeds to read them as such. They comprise several logical, even if stuttering, utterances that culminate in declarative sentences juxtaposed in a cause-effect relationship that leads to implicit or explicit conclusions or that puts in relief the absurdity of earlier statements. The first stanza reads:

> English
> is my mother tongue.
> A mother tongue is not
> not a foreign lan lan lang
> language
> l/anguish
> anguish
> —a foreign anguish.

The poem continues as a repository for the narrator's reflections on the functions of a mother tongue as well as her observations that English fulfils no such function for her. Even so the text in many ways echoes, in a Bakhtinian sense, the voices of the colonial powers. It is moreover written with a seductive lyricism that could easily be associated with the poetry of dominance. In other words, its sound harmonizes with the hegemonic view of things.

But throughout, Philip centres what the reader recognizes as poetic text between two prose passages, the first of which one can only read when the top of the page becomes its side, because it is written in vertical rather than horizontal lines. The adjustment made, the first vertical statement reads:

> WHEN IT WAS BORN, THE MOTHER HELD HER NEWBORN CHILD CLOSE: SHE BEGAN THEN TO LICK IT ALL OVER. THE CHILD WHIMPERED A LITTLE, BUT AS THE MOTHER'S TONGUE MOVED FASTER AND STRONGER OVER ITS BODY, IT GREW SILENT—THE MOTHER TURNING IT THIS WAY AND THAT UNDER HER TONGUE, UNTIL SHE HAD TONGUED IT CLEAN OF THE CREAMY WHITE SUBSTANCE COVERING ITS BODY. (Philip 1989, 56)

The third column, written in the usual left-to-right pattern of English print, begins about one-quarter of the way down the page, and reads:

> Edict I
> Every owner of slaves
> shall, wherever possible,
> ensure that his slaves
> belong to as many ethno-
> linguistic groups as
> possible. If they
> cannot speak to each other,
> they cannot then foment
> rebellion and revolution. (56)

Let us deal with this first page of the poem. Why does the reader move to the middle column? Not to do so means that he will have to change the order of print to which he has become accustomed. Moreover, this is a collection of poems, and his attention is drawn to what he recognizes as having the shape of poetry. When he has read all three columns, he is confronted with concepts and functions of tongues that vary from one culture to another and that diverge still further along the lines of intent even within the same culture. The reader has also listened to several voices, each with a separate agenda. The left column, echoing the ethnographer's voice, records the mother's use, in a non-Occidental culture, of her physical tongue to make her newborn physically acceptable to her, to taste her child literally, but more so to bond the child to herself. The right column contrasts with the left insofar as it is an edict to deprive peoples of their tongues precisely to impede bonding and inflict psychological maiming. But not to be overlooked is the conditioned response to read first what we have been conditioned to think is poetry. The response itself is metonymic of an inexhaustible list of other conditioned responses deriving from imposed tongues.

By the time, therefore, that we have read the first third of what's written in traditional poetic form together with what is found in the margins, the lyrical voices in the centre column have been substantially challenged.

But the next page is discontinuous and provides additional perspectives for understanding how language—all concepts for that matter—derives from and consolidates further the power groups in society. The passage is worth citing in its entirety:

> Those parts of the brain chiefly responsible for speech are named after two learned nineteenth century doctors, the eponymous Doctors Wernicke and Broca respectively.
>
> Dr Broca believed the size of the brain determined intelligence; he devoted much of his time to "proving" that white males of the Caucasian race had larger brains than, and were superior to, women, Blacks and other peoples of colour.
>
> Understanding and recognition of the spoken word takes place in Wernicke's area—the left temporal lobe, situated next to the auditory cortex; from there relevant information passes to Broca's area—situated in the left frontal cortex—which then forms the response and passes it to the motor cortex. The motor cortex controls the muscles of speech. (57)

This is trenchant irony. Implicit here is the notion of language as a tool for instituting lies designed to further empower the reigning hegemony, lies which become part of Occidental epistemology and tools of the hegemonic hermeneutical system used to evaluate and inform all later reality. Language, then, in the guise of science, as implement of oppression and distortion, is chiefly what this passage depicts.

When the reader moves from this history lesson to the next page, the poem in the centre column resumes, and the functions of the tongue continue to be articulated in the left column:

> THE MOTHER THEN PUTS HER FINGERS INTO HER CHILD'S MOUTH—GENTLY FORCING IT OPEN; SHE

> TOUCHES HER TONGUE TO THE CHILD'S TONGUE, AND HOLDING THE TINY MOUTH OPEN, SHE BLOWS INTO IT—HARD. SHE WAS BLOWING WORDS—HER WORDS, HER MOTHER'S WORDS, THOSE OF HER MOTHER'S MOTHER, AND ALL THEIR MOTHERS BEFORE INTO HER DAUGHTER'S MOUTH. (58)

In the right column a second edict, more severe than the first, is enunciated:

> Edict II
> Every slave caught speak-
> ing his native language
> shall be severely pun-
> ished. Where necessary,
> removal of the tongue is
> recommended. The of-
> fending organ, when re-
> moved, should be hung
> on high in a central place,
> so that all may see and tremble. (58)

Thus, on the left are the functions of the tongue, functions that point to the conferring of identity and psychological stability as well as the attaining, understanding, preserving, and transmitting of one's ontology; on the right are edicts prohibiting mothers from possessing a tongue; and in the centre is the speaker vainly essaying to reconcile, in dialectics for which there is no possibility of synthesis, her knowledge that English, while claiming to be her mother, mother's and mothering tongue, traumatizes both her person and the collectivity that informs it.

The seeming confusion here in identifying one's tongue is metonymic of the pathology engendered by colonial practices. Without the prose passages to inform the formally poetic, the readers of "Discourse on the Logic of Language" would be trapped, like the speaker in the middle column, within a maze of conflicting feelings over what constitutes a mothering tongue. But, as regards technique, the insertion of the prose passages, Philip's challenge to TS Eliot's notion of "objective correlative," lacks precedent. Philip says that several publishers to whom she sent the manuscript returned it with long dissertations on what was and wasn't poetry (Philip 1992, 54). But Philip's technique, as practised here, reflects the tradition echoed over and over by the New Black Aesthetic Movement that the Black artist has a responsibility to educate the Black reader.[4]

As the columns nuance or cancel out the information in one another, as one shifts the text physically and the text shifts one historically—back to the colonial edicts that destroyed the tongues of Africans transported in bondage, followed by a return to the narrative of a contemporary descendant of such Africans, back to the origins of the lies that sanction the atrocities of the past and apologize for but do not remedy the oppression of the present—one begins to appreciate the depth and breadth of Philip's technique. One could plausibly say that Philip scrutinizes the pages of Prospero's book, crosses things out and adds much that was left out. This is evident in the poem's final section, which depicts the confusion present in today's African diaspora through a series of simulated multiple-choice questions that link the imposed tongue with evocations of nonsense, rape, bigotry, and brutal oppression but which equally challenge the reader to see more than the imposed meanings in the notion of tongue. The result is that the strategies that readers acquire for decoding poetic texts, for reading the English language as a whole, become useless, for they find themselves in a protean linguistic environment, which serves to evoke, at least partially, the nightmare world of "detongued" slaves in an alien, brutal environment that assaulted every humane principle.

The poem we have just examined depicts why English (and by extrapolation all tongues imposed on members of the African diaspora) is an affliction, how it has sought to annihilate and partially succeeded in transforming African worldviews into a shadowlike reality—analogous with bestiality, lust, brute force, ignorance, and stupidity.

If "Discourse on the Logic of Language" analyzes the lies that enshrine the notion of mother tongue, "Universal Grammar," the poem that immediately follows it, dissects the racist, ethnocentric, and chauvinistic values for which Occidental languages are a vehicle. The narrator begins the poem in the guise of providing a lesson in parsing. What she goes on to do, however, is to show that parsing, as practised in English, masks rather than uncovers the meanings of words. The example she gives to explain parsing advances an ideological position that challenges the very function of parsing:

> **Parsing**—the exercise of telling the part of speech of each word in a sentence (Latin, pars, a part)
>
> **The**—distinguishing adjective, limiting the noun, cell.
>
> **smallest**—adjective of quantity, superlative degree, qualifying the noun cell (unsuccessfully).
>
> **cell**—common noun, neuter gender, singular number, third person, nominative case governing the intransitive verb, remembers (Long-term memory improves cell growth in nerve cells).
>
> **remembers**—regular verb, transitive, active voice, indicative mood, present tense, singular number, third person agreeing with its nominative, cell which remembers and so re-members.
>
> **O**—sound of exclamation as in O God! Made by rounding the lips; first syllable of word name of African goddess of the river—O/shun. (62)

This example further suggests that it is meanings, some denotative but most connotative, that give languages their value. When the speaker's worldview, myths, and values are absent in the national language, as is clearly demonstrated in the examples given throughout *She Tries Her Tongue*, then clearly it is not the speaker's language. In the parentheses as well as in the unbracketed parts of the above definition, the speaker inserts her reality; she subverts the dominant reality, registers Caliban's voice, and undermines Prospero's epistemology.

This is thus both a deconstructive and a reconstructive exercise and sets the scene for the rest of the poem, which is about re-membering (putting the pieces back). The remaining five sections of the poem expand this process in a variety of ways. Let us examine sections two and six (the classification is mine). Section two reads:

> *Man*
> *Man is*
> *The tall man is*

The tall blond man is
The tall, blond, blue-eyed man is
The tall, blond, blue-eyed, white skinned man is

MANY FACTORS AFFECT AND DETERMINE THE ORDER OF WORDS IN A SPOKEN SENTENCE: THE STATE OF MIND OF THE SPEAKER; THE GENDER OF THE SPEAKER; HIS OR HER INTENTIONS; THE CONTEXT OF THE SPEECH; THE IMPRESSION THE SPEAKER WISHES TO MAKE; THE BALANCE OF POWER BETWEEN SPEAKER AND LISTENER AND, NOT LEAST OF ALL, THE CONSTRAINTS OF UNIVERSAL GRAMMAR

The tall blond, blue-eyed, white-skinned man is shooting

the smallest cell
remembers
a sound
(sliding two semitones to return
home)
a secret order
among syllables
Leg/ba
O/shun
Shan/go
heart races
blood pounds
remembers
speech

(63)

For convenience, let us call each transition in this section a stanza. If we consider the observation made by several critics, notably Roland Barthes, that the European bourgeoisie imposed its own values on reality and thereafter employed its power to impress its reality upon the rest of the world as universal truths (32-33), the second stanza (the prose passage) that interrupts the first with statements about the relativity and arbitrariness in the meaning of language is particularly pertinent. This passage assaults meaning here and may even defeat Philip's purpose, if the reader were to interpret it according to Philip's criteria. Still it is worthwhile to note that the first stanza is narrated in rhythms that evoke the African tom-tom (which is reminiscent of the heartbeat responding to various emotions). The stanza builds cumulatively from the single word "man" to the last line: "The tall, blond, blue-eyed, white-skinned man is," and is an accretion that mocks the principles of parsing. But Philip arranges the words so that the passage resembles a triangular blade. Up to this point the italicized stanza, except for rhythm and shape, is innocuous. But rhythm and shape are not innocuous and are therefore potent tropes, especially because an absence of faith in the veracity of the "word" is the thematic nucleus of the poem.

The interrupting prose passage not only throws a shadow on meaning but becomes a barrier between the first stanza and its displaced concluding line. This strategy on Philip's part is certainly not whimsicality, for it comments on the creative and functional uses of language. The fracturing of the first stanza with a list of the impediments that impact on meaning in language drives a wedge into the notion that language is a unifying force. In this regard, we think of Barthes's injunction to the writer to employ those means by which "literature becomes the receptacle of existence in all its density" (32). By inviting the reader to reflect on the state of mind of the narrator, her gender, and intentions, the phenomena that critics of the autotelic schools discourage their colleagues from examining, the narrator also challenges certain dogmas that limit the interpretation of literature and thus enshrine an unchallenged, hegemonic discourse.

The choice of "shooting" in the solitary line fragmented from the first stanza to further expand "man" moves the meanings in a totally new direction, for prior to this we have only an amalgam of noun, adjectives, and the copulative verb *is*. Violence, death, power are quickly evoked in our minds. If the readers are nonwhite, the words evoke the history of colonial conquest and its continuing legacy. If they are white, it may well evoke the sense of conqueror, feelings of racial supremacy, or feelings of guilt or combinations of all three. Again, as we attempt to make an interpretation, we keep an uneasy eye on the prose passage, which mocks our interpretive efforts. We are still ignorant of the shooting man's targets when Philip disrupts the text to inscribe elements of re-membering.

Because of its positioning, the re-membering passage is to some extent the object of "shooting." And it is only on the surface that this notion appears absurd, for if we remember "Edict II" of the previous poem, we realize that one objective of the infliction of pain by the white master was to detongue the slave, to remove even the remotest possibility of preserving or regenerating the slave's mother tongue. Yet, according to the narrator, the language survives in "a secret order" embodied in the African deities of "Leg/ba, O/shun, Shango." If we turn our thoughts to the cults that sprang up in the African diaspora around these figures, we may see that Philip is acknowledging the failure of the slavemaster to root out the slave's tongue. This reader is reminded of Edouard Glissant's observation that another language had to be forged, a language independent of the one the planter sought to impose, to endure the atrocities of plantation life; it is a language that too eventually supplants the planters' (77-89). Legba, shape-changing trickster, mediator between humans and deities in Africa, became John, Anansi, Brer Rabbit in the slave cultures of the West and thus a vital part of the mythic and existential apparatus of the slaves. Shango, the Yoruba deity of storms, whose cults exist even today in Trinidad, Grenada, Haiti, Brazil, and elsewhere in other names, is a vital force in the creation of life. He was a vital force in the maintenance of a worldview independent of that imposed by the slavemaster. If these survived, then there still exist the germs, the speaker poignantly hints, for the re-membering, the re-invention of mothering tongues. Hence the excitement embodied in words that continue, at another level, to mock parsing as a way of analyzing language and to foreground the absurdity we oftentimes ignore in the many masks of language. The speaker as Caliban and Legba is enjoying herself in this new linguistic maze that is not Prospero's terrain.

Part six of the poem, its concluding section, reads:

> when the smallest cell remembers—
> how do you
> how can you
> when the smallest cell
>
> remembers
>
> lose a language

O homen alto, louro de olhos azuis está a disparar
El blanco rubio, alto de ojos azules está disparando
De lange, blanke, blonde man, met der blauwe ogen, is aan het schieten
Le grand homme blanc et blond aux yeux bleus tire sur
Der grosser weisse mann, blonde mit bleuen augen hatgeschossen
The tall, blond, blue-eyed, white-skinned man is shooting

an elephant
a native
a wild animal
a Black
a woman
a child

somewhere.

Slip mouth over syllable; moisten with tongue the word. Suck slide Play Caress Blow—Love it, but if the word gags, does not nourish, bite it off
—at its source—
Spit it out
Start again

(67)

The first six lines reiterate what we have already seen. Their value lies chiefly in establishing in the reader's mind that the poem is a cleansing ritual for the trauma caused by the imposed language. But we also hear in them the voice of the spiritual guide who, in neo-African religions of New World—the religions that sanctify Legba, Shango, Ogun, and Oshun—accompanies and reassures the seeker during the quest for self-enlightenment.

The translation into five additional languages—Portuguese, Spanish, Dutch, French, and German—of the shooting statement serves two functions: to demonstrate how a concept accommodates badly from one language to another, and to show that, linguistic difficulties aside, the end product is the same: whether the man obliterates the thing or person or whether he shoots it, the result is death.

When the multiple object is furnished for the verb "is shooting," a uniform value scale, achieved through zeugma, is applied to elephant, native, wild animal, woman, child. Moreover, the tense employed is the continuous present. This suggests quite the opposite reality of what the West terms "The White Man's Burden." In a certain sense it stands Kiplingesque reality—the official European and Euro-American mythology—on its head. This is "enlightenment" from the barrel of a gun, moreover, a gun whose user does not care to discriminate among the targets. Putting the victims' history into poetic form is what Philip is doing, for the passage evokes the systematic massacres undertaken against the world's non-European indigenous peoples (Brown 148-74), the horrors of apartheid, the extermination of ethnic groups such as the Tainos in the Greater Antilles, not to mention the forced transportation of people to work stolen land, to be roasted, packed with gunpowder and blown to bits, . . . when they resisted the colonizers' intentions (Lamming 98-99). The present continuous tense is apt, for it reminds us of the ongoing devastating psychological processes engendered by colonial practices (Fanon; Grier and Cobb; Poussaint).

Needless to say, if blond is beautiful in the European's mother tongue, it is bestial in the continental and diasporic African's, i e, in Caliban's tongues. One way of regaining (or fashioning) a mother tongue is to create a language vested with one's memories, one's history, one's own story, in which blond cannot but be bestial. Being the target of the European's pistol is a determining aspect of the history of nonwhite peoples. But it is a story distorted by hegemonic European and Euro-American discourse, a narrative that still largely represents the white man as saviour and the native and nonwhite as dangerous and incompetent.

Still employing the technique of zeugma, Philip establishes an analogy between rape and a dehumanizing tongue, and offers a single solution for both—biting off the offending word or organ and spitting it out, and therefore advocates radical destruction rather than cosmetic changes. Similarly, the passage advocates those revolutionary changes nonwhite writers must make to the inherited colonial languages which are often their only mode of communication.

It is easy to infer from the content of these poems as well as from their arrangement that Philip brings a clearly and carefully worked out ideology to poetry. For example, one begins the composition by first focusing on the weight of history attached to the word. There is no value in a language that transmogrifies its user. If the only available language dehumanizes its user, then a substantial part of the writer's mission is to rid the language of its pathological content. In my interview with Philip she explained that, having understood how the word as traditionally used undergirds and sanctifies oppression, she could no longer write traditional poetry (Thomas 2006, 203). This explains why her work evinces scorn for pure forms, why several discourses come together and even clash in her texts; for selected discourse, the oppressor being the arbiter has always meant the silencing of the oppressed.

Principles of autotelianism or not, critics have not taken kindly to Ms Philip's deconstruction of the concepts sacrosanct to English culture. Her collection of essays *Frontiers* documents many of the battles her approaches to poetry have incited, and the methods the purveyors of hegemonic discourse have employed to silence her.

Before concluding, it may be prudent to state that many Caribbean writers—Derek Walcott or John Hearne, for example—would disagree with many aspects of Philip's portrayal of English. One might add that writers of equal significance—Earl Lovelace, Patrick Chamoiseau, Edouard Glissant—agree with many of her arguments.[5] However, while these issues are thematically relevant to Philip's poetry, we have not the space to explore them here. Suffice it to say that her poetry points to and sets in place some of the processes by which Africans of the diaspora could create an identity from the vestiges of an African past—from the debris of colonial psychological pillage—and expunge from their psyches much of the camouflaged but crippling freight of self-inferiority and self-hatred. If there is a criticism to be made, it may be one that Walcott warns about in "The Muse of History," to the effect that art created along such guidelines risks being reduced entirely to contesting the lies propagated by European and Euro-America discourse about the world's nonwhite peoples (2).

Philip states in her interview that she writes in several forms to make her writing reflect "the mess and the morass and the matrix" out of which it comes (Thomas 2006, 204-205). Like several of the writers of the Black Arts Movement and continental Africa, she sees herself as someone committed to splitting open the lies by which the Occident obfuscates reality (198). One way is to start "reconstructing the language that surrounds us . . . Instead of aid to Africa, let's start talking about reparations to Africa . . . instead of women and power, let's talk about women and theft—then let's talk some more about compensation for that theft" (Philip 1992, 77).

This is an updated and revised version of an essay bearing the same title that was published in Studies of the Literary Imagination *(Vol xxvi, No 2) Fall 1993.*

ROHINTON MISTRY

"Beggaring the Nation": Bodily Inscription and the Body Politic in Rohinton Mistry's *A Fine Balance*

James W Johnson

Drawing from his briefcase "a large sketchbook containing his notes and diagrams on the dramaturgy of begging," the Beggarmaster in Rohinton Mistry's *A Fine Balance* displays before Dina, Ishvar, Om, and Maneck an "old pencil drawing" titled the "Spirit of Collaboration": "Two figures, one sitting aloft on the shoulders of the other" (Mistry 1995, 437). "For this," he explains, "I need a lame beggar and a blind beggar. The blind man will carry the cripple on his shoulders. A living, breathing image of the ancient story about friendship and cooperation. And it will produce a fortune in coins . . . because people will not only give from pity or piety, but also from admiration" (437). Although this is one of several passages from the novel in which the Beggarmaster, the powerful "manager" of Bombay's begging industry, describes the disfigured bodies of Bombay's beggars in terms of their potential profitability, this particular proposal is especially revealing. In it, bodies figure not only as the material evidence of suffering and privation but also as symbols that garner both pity and admiration through their ability to signify and tell a story. The reliance of the Beggarmaster's scheme on the embodiment of meaning points to the broader function of the corporeal. Indeed, Mistry's pervasive use of bodily metaphor and description reveals a fundamental concern with the representational capacity of the body, a capacity that is the result not of dramaturgical deliberation but of the historical and political processes of bodily inscription.

A number of scholars have registered the ubiquity of bodily metaphor and description in the fiction of Mistry. John Eustace offers a compelling argument for understanding the evacuative body and excremental representations in Mistry's short story "Squatter" as generating "a positive political valency" (2003, 2). Examining Keynesian economics in *A Fine Balance*, Tyler Tokaryk offers a short but intriguing Bakhtinian reading of the grotesque body; he asserts that the individual body in Mistry's work is subjected to "forces that transform it into a perverse analogue of the system of development economics" (2005, 21). Similarly, in his critical biography *Rohinton Mistry* (2004), Peter Morey gestures toward the broader relationship between individual bodies and the body politic in *A Fine Balance*: "the bodily distress of the characters appears also that of the city they inhabit—and perhaps of the body politic more generally" (102). In spite of the wide critical recognition of the significance of the body in Mistry's fiction, however, only Morey has undertaken a direct critical treatment of the corporeal in that novel. In his article "Terrible Beautification: Body Politics in Rohinton Mistry's *A Fine Balance* (2001)," he examines the allegorical significance of the body. Drawing on Frederic Jameson's concept of "national allegory," Morey uses the novel to argue for "a more dynamic and cumulative" understanding of national allegories in India. "Individual texts," argues Morey, "are not in themselves self-contained allegories for the Indian nation" (2001, 75). Although he offers numerous compelling perspectives on the function of the body in the novel, including the potential for the body "to bear the signs of ethnic allegiance," he provides no sustained analysis of the body as the site of historical and political processes of inscription (76). Nor does Morey explore the fundamental contradiction that undermines the Indira Gandhi regime in the novel, a regime that attempts to eliminate the abject bodies of its constitutive subjects while producing those abject bodies through its disciplinary methods and regulatory practices. Nonetheless, his recognition of the capacity of the body to bear signifying marks invites further critical analysis of Mistry's representations of bodies as inscriptive surfaces.

In *A Fine Balance*, recurrent images of deteriorating bodies create patterns that underwrite the narrative's cohesion and chart its progression. Mistry's representations of the body as an inscriptive surface problematize the attempts of the Indira Gandhi regime to depict the Indian body politic as a coherent, homogeneous, and corporeal totality. Images of deteriorating bodies, the production of docile bodies, and real and imagined instances of infestation and infection all contribute to a disjunction between official representations of the body politic and the images of individual bodies that populate Mistry's India. Thus, against the dominant state-sponsored narrative of bodily health, purity, and homogeneity, Mistry offers a complex representation of India during the 1975-77 State of Emergency as a heterogeneous aggregation of interrelated but unique subjects whose bodies are operated upon by the destructive regulatory practices of the Indira Gandhi regime.

Mistry's complex representation of the corporeal readily lends itself to a critical examination attentive to scholarly discourse surrounding the narrative and symbolic functions of the body. The work of Peter Brooks, which examines the capacity of the body within the text—the narrative body—to convey meaning, offers an apposite framework for an investigation of bodily inscription in Mistry's fiction. Conceiving of bodies as inscriptive surfaces, Brooks (1993) provides a basis for exploring the body in *A Fine Balance* as the site of historical and political processes that inscribe the bodies on which they operate. When resulting from the deliberate actions of the state, the same processes can be understood to correspond with what Michel Foucault calls "disciplines." These disciplinary processes manifest themselves in the novel as the policies and actions undertaken by the Indian government during the State of Emergency. The purpose and result of these regulatory practices are the production of what Foucault calls "docile bodies"—bodies that are both useful and obedient. However, in attempting to produce docile bodies, the same processes dismember, disfigure, and deform the bodies that they target. In turn, these seemingly imperfect bodies contrast with the political body, or body politic, depicted by the government. This body politic comprises a social structure that, according to Elizabeth Grosz, assumes a "hierarchical organization" modelled on the "(presumed and projected) structure of the body" (1999, 384). Disrupting the coherence and stability of this social structure by challenging its cogency, the inscribed bodies of India's disenfranchised can thus be identified with Julia Kristeva's concept of the "abject body." Accordingly, the proliferation of abject bodies in the text and the perceived threat of overpopulation are evidence of the transgressive power that Kristeva identifies with abjection, that which "does not respect borders, positions, or rules" (1982, 4). These theorists provide a valuable theoretical apparatus through which to explore the inscribed and abject bodies of India's subaltern in Mistry's novel.

In the wake of renewed interest in the concept of the body as an analytical tool in Western discourse, various theorists have sought to unsettle its usage in the analysis of non-Western societies. Use of the body as an analytical tool, they argue, is largely the result of wider beliefs in Western culture and of Western capitalism in particular (Turner 2001, 93). Such critics suggest that by "adopting the body as an interpretive tool in South Asia the investigator is simply exporting a cultural product of late twentieth-century Western society—the obsession with the body—to the non-West" (Mills and Sen 2004, 2-3). However, Mills and Sen respond to this criticism by stressing the historical and social significance of the corporeal in South Asia. A wholesale rejection of the body as a means of analyzing India, they argue, "is mistaken for the simple reason that the body was at the heart of systems of society, of metaphor, and of identity in South Asia long before Europeans came to have an impact in the region, and certainly long before Western academics began to explore concepts of the corporeal" (4). Moreover, it would be a mistake to presume that the differences between Western and non-Western conceptions of the body preclude an analysis based on Western theories of the corporeal. As Mills and Sen observe, "the ways in which South Asian communities have used their bodies to construct notions of rank, difference and gender and the extent to which they have made them social surfaces resemble activities in other societies, and comparative study may cast light upon all these processes" (6). Indeed, beyond viewing the body as an object for the discursive processes of social organization, the body in India has been seen "to provide a surface on which the whole world of messages [is] encoded and presented" (5). This concept of the body as inscriptive surface is one to which later Western theorists such as Brooks, Foucault, Kristeva, and Grosz have dedicated a great deal of theoretical attention. Rather than rejecting the work of Western theorists on the basis of dissimilarities, then, I will explore the body through the work of these theorists with the conviction that affinities between Western and non-Western conceptions of the body offer a productive ground on which to formulate a critical exploration of the body in the work of Rohinton Mistry.

For Mistry, the body is made meaningful through narrative, but the narrative also gains coherence through its incorporation of the somatic. Indeed, the integration of corporeality into the narrative underpins its structure and progression. As *A Fine Balance* begins, the sudden lurch of the train on which Ishvar, Om, and Maneck are travelling sends their bodies crashing into one another, propelling the reader into the narrative and introducing three of the novel's four protagonists: the rural-born, Dalit tailors Ishvar Darji and his nephew Omkaprash "Om" Darji, and Maneck Kolah, a young Parsi student who has come to Bombay to study. The physical description of these characters is the first in a succession of bodily images that proliferate as the novel progresses. As the narrative shifts its focus from this early encounter to the history of Dina Dalal, a widowed seamstress who eventually hires Ishvar and Om and lodges Maneck, the deterioration and destruction of bodies begin to feature prominently. In the second part of the novel, the slow and steady physical deterioration of Dina's mother is soon followed by the death of her grandfather, commencing a pattern of bodily deterioration that includes Dina's diminishing eyesight, the aging proofreader and former lawyer Vasantro Valmik's waning vocal cords, and the rent collector Ibrahim's increasing feebleness. The lurid details of the death of Dina's husband, Rustom Dalal, his "head completely crushed" after being hit by a "bastard lorry driver" (43), similarly begin a pattern of traffic accidents.

In addition to charting a figurative course along which the narrative progresses, bodily decline evidences forms of bodily inscription that operate alternatively along the lines of caste and class. Outside the urban centres of Mistry's India, it is almost exclusively the bodies of Dalit Indians that function as sites of violence. Ishvar; his father, Dukhi Mochi; his brother, Narayan; and his mother, Roopa, are untouchables by virtue of having been born into the Chaamar caste of leather workers. In the rural village in which they live, the Dalit body inscribed by the violence inflicted by upper-caste members serves as a signifier of caste membership. According to Mills and Sen, "The organization of caste and rank provides important evidence [of the body as an object of social organization] . . . and the manifestation and centre of 'purity' and 'untouchability'" (4). Mistry's description of the caste system confronted by Dukhi and his family serves to undermine such notions of bodily purity. Identified with the rotting entrails and excrement of dead animals, "the ethos of the caste system" itself is depicted in *A Fine Balance* as fundamentally impure.

For Dukhi and his sons, caste differentiation is discernible by the staining and strong odour of their skin that result from leather working, "the trade to which they were born shackled" (101). The inevitable inscription of their bodies under the caste system thus reveals a contradiction that undermines Mahatma Gandhi's dual commitment to abolition of untouchability and preservation of the caste system. For Gandhi, "untouchability is the product, not of the caste system, but of the distinction of high and low"; thus, "the moment untouchability goes, the caste system itself will be purified" (Gandhi 1977, 261). Asserting that the caste system "lends itself easily to reform," Gandhi in his essay "Brahmacharya" nevertheless maintained that the purity of the body is a precondition for the purity of the caste system (1951, 172). As Maneck later relates in *A Fine Balance* when quoting Gandhi to his activist friend Avinash, Gandhi "believed firmly in cleanliness—physical purity precedes mental purity precedes spiritual purity" (242). However, because of their membership in the untouchable Chaamar caste, Dukhi and his family are unable to meet the basic standard of physical "cleanliness" necessary for "spiritual purity." Furthermore, whipping and dismemberment, punishments for perceived insolence and the transgression of caste lines leave unmistakable marks upon the bodies of the lower castes, whichbear witness to the regulatory practices employed by upper-caste members. Mistry's portrayal of these regulatory practices evinces the production of "docile bodies." "In every society," writes Foucault, "the body was in the grip of very strict powers, which imposed on it constraints, prohibitions or obligations" (1991, 263). A body is docile so "that it may be subjected, used, transformed and improved" (263). The rules governing the types of labour that they are allowed to perform, and the punishments exacted for inefficiency, also render the bodies of the Chaamars useful and obedient.

As the narrative shifts from the rural village by the river to the city of Bombay, adherence to the rigidity of the caste system diminishes, but the regulatory practices of authoritarianism do not. In Bombay, it is not strictly the lower castes but the lower classes more generally that are subjected to the regulatory practices that operate on, and consequently inscribe, the body. The marks left on the bodies of the disenfranchised as a result of forced sterilization, part of the government's "family planning" program implemented to combat overpopulation, are evident not only in the scars left by the specific vasectomy and tubal ligation operations but also in the resulting complications, such as the amputation of Ishvar's legs as the result of an infection caused by the vasectomy and Om's castration, which not only removes his ability to have children but also drastically alters his bodily schema. Once thin and nimble, by the novel's epilogue Om has become overweight and lumbering. Directed at Bombay's indigent slum and pavement dwellers, the government's "family planning initiative" imprints itself principally on the bodies of India's lower classes.

It is the Beggarmaster's industry of beggary that comprises the novel's most extreme example of somatic docility. Not only does the Beggarmaster transform already disfigured bodies into docile bodies by maximizing their potential to evoke pity, but also he creates disfigurements by manipulating the bodies of the healthy. Infants and young children, such as the niece and nephew of the Monkeyman, a street performer who lives in the same Bombay slum as Ishvar and Om, are sent away for "professional modification" (447). These modifications, however, are nothing more than horrific mutilations. After being caught sleeping in the streets by the police, Ishvar, Om, and a large group of pavement dwellers are rounded up and driven to a rural construction site, part of the government's irrigation project, where they are forced to perform hard labour. As the tailors are driven out of Bombay to the irrigation project, Shankar, the Beggarmaster's most prized and severely disfigured beggar, describes to Ishvar and Om the relationship between mutilation and profit: "[P]utting a baby's eyes out will automatically earn money. Blind beggars are everywhere. But blind with eyeballs missing, face showing empty sockets, plus nose chopped off—now anyone will give money for that" (323). The clinical vocabulary adopted by the Beggarmaster, in addition to his meticulous study and documentation of the relationship between the beggars' bodies and their profitability, provides a paradigmatic instance of manufactured docility. Furthermore, though the begging industry predates the State of Emergency, the emphasis on discipline and commerce by state authorities during that period allows for the institutionalization of the Beggarmaster's enterprise.

According to Tokaryk, Mistry's novel is forthright about presenting "the begging industry . . . as the effect . . . of a number of complex social, economic, and political discourses—the same discourses that generate such generous profits for Nusswan and other members of the economic elite" (2005, 24). Although the Beggarmaster's business most clearly illustrates how the practices justified by this discourse inscribe the bodies of those whom it subjugates, his use and manipulation of bodies parallel the broader initiatives undertaken by India's economic and political elite during the State of Emergency. Accordingly, the actions of both private industry and the state illustrate an attempt to perfect the production of docility through the use of what Foucault calls "disciplines," the "methods which made possible the meticulous control of the operations of the body" and assured "the constant subjection of its forces" (1991, 262). In *A Fine Balance*, Bombay's slum dwellers are corralled into buses and driven out to a rural political rally against their will, they are forced to sit silently through countless speeches extolling the virtues of the State of Emergency. Although the vast majority of attendees are there unwillingly, the sycophantic member of parliament for the district calls on the journalists to "observe: wherever the Prime Minister goes, thousands gather from miles around to see her and hear her. Surely this is the mark of a truly great leader" (261). The bodies of those in attendance have been made useful through their mere presence.

When Indira Gandhi finally speaks, her message is telling: "The need of the hour is discipline—discipline in every aspect of life" (263). The reluctant spectators give little thought to the prime minister's instruction, but those whose interests are directly served by the docility of the underclass enthusiastically endorse Gandhi's aphorisms. Mrs Gupta, Dina's employer and the owner of Au Revoir Exports, is among those entrepreneurs who frequently parrot the prime minister's precepts: "'The

Need of the Hour Is Discipline'—that's the Prime Minister's message on the poster. . . . It wouldn't be a bad idea to stick a few posters on the Au Revoir entrance" (74). Although her injunction for discipline seems to be strictly verbal, her support for state-sponsored sterilization and forced labour makes her complicit in those practices that abuse the bodies of India's subaltern: "Thank God the Prime Minister has taken firm steps" (74). Ironically, the marks left on the body by these disciplinary methods undermine the efficacy of the state's regulatory practice, for these "docile" bodies are ultimately perceived as a threat to the social stability of India. In addition to preserving authoritarian systems of control and exploitation, the subjugation of individual bodies in the State of Emergency is an attempt to separate a conception of the nation as body from its individual constitutive subjects. In her article "Bodies-Cities," Elizabeth Grosz argues that "the body politic, whatever form it may take, justifies and naturalizes itself with reference to some form of hierarchical organization modelled on the (presumed and projected) structure of the body" (1999, 46). Thus, the Indira Gandhi regime employs the corporeal rhetoric of cleanliness and beauty in order to depict the marked and often disfigured body of the subaltern as a threat to the purity of the Indian body politic.

Leaders from the Indian National Congress are the first in Mistry's novel to depict the Indian body politic as a corporeal body in need of purification in a speech to rural village dwellers: "How can we begin to be strong when there is a disease in our midst? First we must be rid of this disease that plagues the body of our motherland" (107). After the subsequent ascent of Indira Gandhi and the declaration of the State of Emergency, the same metaphors of infection and purgation are used to justify the project of beautification, a government program aimed at "beautifying" the city of Bombay. Slogans such as "FOOD FOR THE HUNGRY! HOMES FOR THE HOMELESS!" and "THE NATION IS ON THE MOVE!" present an ironic facade for the destruction of Bombay's slums and the removal of beggars and pavement dwellers from the city (299).

According to Morey, Mistry's depiction of slum clearances and mass sterilization serves as an indictment against "a body politic, which attempts to perfect the larger body of India by getting rid of its anonymous imperfect bodies and preventing their proliferation" (2001, 182). Morey's description of the body politic "ridding" itself of countless unwanted and "anonymous imperfect bodies," a description that sounds like pest control, is particularly apt given Mistry's preoccupation with infestation, parasitism, and infection. The poisonous centipedes along the edge of the Bombay slum where Ishvar and Om live, the bedbugs that Maneck encounters when he first arrives at the college hostel in Bombay, and the lice that Dina notices on Om's scalp are a few of the novel's more prominent images of infestation. One of the earliest significant encounters with pests occurs when Maneck first washes himself in Dina's bathroom after moving to her house from the college hostel. Peering around the bathing area, he is disgusted at the sight of worms "crawling out of the drain in formidable numbers, stringy and dark red, glistening on the grey stone floor, advancing with their mesmeric glide" (200).

In addition to recalling the already prevalent representations of decay and death, the worms that Maneck encounters in Dina's bathroom prefigure later images of parasitism. Within the first week of the tailors' arrival at her house, Dina begins to suspect that Om is infected with worms: "apart from Omkaprash's skinniness . . . she frequently spied his fingers relieving an itch in his fundament; and that, she felt, was evidence as conclusive as any" (79). Her suggestion becomes a source of humour for most of the novel, but after her suspicion "wriggle[s] out again" she purchases a purge for Om, and her suspicions are proven correct. The "small snake" that emerges from him "wriggling madly" is viewed with comical derision: "That wicked creature and its children were eating up your nourishment. Hundreds of stomachs within your stomach" (465). The government's adoption of similar terms of infestation and purgation to describe removal of the marginalized beggars and pavement dwellers of Bombay, however, is given a far more solemn association. If, as Grosz suggests, the presumed structure of the body provides a model for how hierarchical social structures are organized, then the discourse of infestation situates the bodies of the disenfranchised both in opposition to and within the bodily structure—parasites to be purged.

The numerous instances of real infestation in the novel parallel the government's characterization of a pestilence perceived to be afflicting the body politic. The density and proximity of bodies littering the streets of Bombay reinforces the sense of infestation fostered by government discourse: "The pavement dwellers began emerging through the gathering dusk. . . . Within minutes, huddled bodies had laid claim to the concrete. Pedestrians now adapted to the new topography, picking their way carefully through the field of arms and legs and faces" (307). It is in response to this "invasion" of the streets—an invasion that is the direct result of the government's slum clearances—that the government initiates its project of urban "beautification."

Beautifying and purging the city of its dispossessed and destitute residents are part of a broader project aimed at population control. The government's sterilization project is framed as a cure for a potentially fatal affliction of the body politic. Speaking to his assistant, the administrator of one forced sterilization camp advises that "We have to be firm with the doctors. If it is left to them to fight the menace of the population explosion, the nation will drown, choked to death, finished. . . . So it's up to us to make sure the war is won" (523). Situated within a discourse of pathology, India's destitute become the target of a violence framed by official discourse as an eradication of a virulent disease endemic to India.

As bodies that contest and challenge the social order of Indian society under the State of Emergency, the disfigured and deformed bodies of the subaltern in *A Fine Balance* can be identified with what Julia Kristeva calls "abject bodies." In her seminal work *Powers of Horror: An Essay on Abjection* (1982), Kristeva formulates a theory of abjection in which the abject body, degraded and debased, offers a form of resistance. The abject is "what disturbs identity, system, order. What does not respect borders, positions, rules" (4). Kristeva's assertion of the transgressive properties of the abject body is variously confirmed throughout Mistry's novel. The government is unable to effectively control the abject bodies that its own regulatory practices have produced. The frustration of Bombay's policemen during the funeral march for Shankar at the end of the novel is especially revelatory of the capacity of abject bodies to defy state power. Attempting to speed up a procession of beggars, Bombay's traffic constables are at a loss when their disciplinary methods fail to evoke a response: "[T]hey waved their arms, tooted their whistles, shouted and pleaded, gesticulated, grimaced, clutched their foreheads and shook their fists. But these tried and true methods were employed in vain: absent limbs could not respond no matter how piercing the whistle or vigorous the wave" (495).

The threat to state control created by the presence of abject bodies is not confined to specific instances in which they appear. More broadly, abjection contests the circumscribed area of the state itself. Abject bodies are conceived of as being "outside" or discrete from the Indian body politic even while being geographically located in the heart of Bombay. As that which transgresses borders, their proliferation threatens to overwhelm the well-defined boundaries of the nation-state, portending what one administrator suspects will be "the end of our civilization" (523). The fear of overpopulation expressed throughout the text thus becomes the fear of an infestation from within and the dissolution of the borders that define the nation-state itself.

To rationalize the discourse of infection and infestation used to justify the extermination of abject bodies, the government must depict the body politic as otherwise healthy and formidable.

The irrigation project exposes the contradictions underlying the government's beautification scheme. While the project's facilitator decries the "beautification police" for indiscriminately corralling disfigured and immobile beggars, the work that the beggars are forced to perform at the irrigation project results in their incapacitation. Furthermore, by forcing the city's beggars into unpaid work, the government displaces the paid workers previously responsible for the irrigation project, leaving them unemployed. Thus, in addition to symbolically "beggaring the nation" by degrading its ecological and geographical body, the government's policies are literally "beggaring the nation" by contributing to the proliferation of impoverished citizens (296). These contradictions reveal how the regulatory practices under the State of Emergency produce the abject body that the hegemon attempts to efface. Yet this production of the abject body is also the inscription of marginalized bodies, whose scars serve as an indictment against proclamations of progress, growth, and purity in official representations of the Indian body politic.

The physical embodiment of these contradictions culminates with the sudden exposure of Shankar's dismembered and mutilated corpse. Initially covered by a "sheet . . . and a blanket of fresh flowers," his severed appendages are scattered across the street when a small contingent of riot police attacks the beggar's funeral procession: "They were mistaken for political activists in fancy dress—troublemakers indulging in street theater, portraying government figures as crooks and criminals intent on beggaring the nation" (296). The procession was never intended to make such a statement, nor is it the result of the Beggarmaster's dramaturgy. Nevertheless, the mistake is a testament to the power of bodies not only to signify but also to offer a potentially oppositional resistance to the hegemony of state discourse. If the abject body is the manifestation of state corruption, then the sudden exposure of Shankar's disarticulated form challenges the totalizing national discourse that posits the homogeneity and purity of the body politic.

According to Anuradha Kapur, "There is in India an unstated problem of depicting an Indian body intra-culturally, that is, in terms of the internal differences that fissure any totalising sense of the nation" (2005, 137). Mistry, however, posits an alternative conception of place that eschews uniformity and absoluteness. In *A Fine Balance*, when Ishvar and Om first arrive at her apartment, Dina views them with suspicion: their "inch long nails," Ishvar's "disfigured cheek," and Om's "skeletal figure, sharp and angular," become sources of suspicion and concern (75). As the stories that these inscriptions provoke are borne out in the narrative, however, her concern about the completion of the clothing orders is subordinated to her genuine concern for the well-being of the tailors: "she read the deterioration in their haggard faces[, and she] feared for their health" (305). For Brooks, "the sign imprints the body, making it part of the signifying process," and "it is the body marked in a significant moment of the person's past history that enables recognition" (1993, 3). In *A Fine Balance*, the initial recognition enabled by the presence of the sign on the body gives way to the disclosure of narrative and to the sharing of the individual histories signified by inscribed bodies. The tragedy that befalls the protagonists of the novel seems to challenge Vasantro Valmik's claim that "to share the story redeems everything" (Mistry 594). Nevertheless, the potential for individuals to establish meaningful relationships across cultural, ethnic, and religious divisions through the sharing of their stories seems to suggest an alternative to either the homogeneous totality endorsed by official representations of

India under the State of Emergency or the fissured and fractured body politic described by Kapur. Rather, Mistry seems to suggest that it is only through an awareness of the diffuse interrelationships among individual subjects that we can begin to imagine the complex and heterogeneous network of linkages of which the nation is comprised.

This is an updated and revised version of "'Beggaring the Nation': Bodily Inscription and the Body Politic in Rohinton Mistry's A Fine Balance,*" previously published in* Studies in Canadian Literature, *Volume 40, Number 1, University of New Brunswick, 2015.*

HIROMI GOTO

Diasporic Violences, Uneasy Friendships, and Hiromi Goto's *The Kappa Child*

Christine Kim

In her landmark essay, "Against the Lures of Diaspora" (1993), Rey Chow makes an argument for increased critical self-reflexivity, particularly from diasporic critics who must be conscious of their own self-interested positioning vis-à-vis China. The essay concludes with a warning:

> Any attempt to deal with "women" or the "oppressed classes" in the "third world" that does not at the same time come to terms with the historical conditions of its own articulation is bound to repeat the exploitativeness that used to and still characterizes most "exchanges" between "West" and "East." Such attempts will also be expediently assimilated within the plenitude of the hegemonic establishment, with all the rewards that that entails. No one can do without some such rewards. What one can do without is the illusion that, through privileged speech, one is helping to save the wretched of the earth. (119)

The diasporic critic may be tempted to conflate her position with those in China and speak from a minoritized position, but this tendency overlooks the significant symbolic and material differences between those located in the West and those in China. Chow urges diasporic critics to be conscious of the relative privilege they possess and the hegemonic positions they occupy, and underlines the need for this cultural capital to be used responsibly, "not merely to speak as exotic minors, but to fight the crippling effects of Western imperialism and Chinese paternalism at once" (114).

Chow's castigating comments about diasporic critics may seem like an odd place to begin an essay about trickster figures, but her urging of intellectuals to take seriously their ethical responsibilities is one that I want to try to heed in this paper. At the same time, Chow's reminder that those of us linked to the Asian diaspora must be conscious of "the historical conditions" of our articulations is also a useful way to enter into a conversation about the relations between diasporic and First Nations communities in Canada. This essay was initially conceived as an attempt to think about Hiromi Goto's representation of the kappa, a creature from Japanese folklore, alongside Indigenous tricksters within Canada. In this way, *The Kappa Child* (2001) forces its readers to take seriously the ethical and political responsibilities of Asian diasporic communities in Canada, and, more specifically, to consider what those responsibilities toward Indigenous communities might be. These are not easy questions, but through its writing of the encounters between the unnamed narrator, a Nisei or second-generation Japanese Canadian, with a kappa, Goto's novel draws attention to issues of history, the occupation of land, and the nature of knowledge, in order to begin working through the difficult positioning of diasporas within structures of settler colonialism.

Forced Occupations, Unwilling Migrations

For fairly self-evident reasons, diasporia studies often demonstrates a preoccupation with issues of movement, migration, and (dis)location. Goto's novel returns us to this familiar ground but treads it with a somewhat different set of destinations in mind. Early on in the novel, the narrator makes the trek back to her parents' home, somewhere vaguely southeast of Lethbridge, Alberta, for Easter. The return to her childhood, enacted literally through the drive back from Calgary, is replayed symbolically during the disastrous holiday dinner. When the narrator's father erupts in a fit of rage over a minor mishap, the responses of the four sisters and their mother make it clear that the father is not the only one trapped in a "pattern so ingrained he can't stop" (27). The narrator's three sisters respond by fleeing the scene and bursting into angry tears, the mother by passively enduring the spectacle, and the narrator by cleaning up the remnants of the dinner that her mother toiled to prepare while thinking to herself that although the girls have now grown into adulthood, their return to their parents' house compels them to "slip into our childhood roles. No one is exempt. Until death do us part" (28).

The text returns repeatedly to this pessimistic view of being unable to escape the violent patterns that characterize the past, on the levels of family interactions, painful friendships, and national history, perhaps in hopes of disproving the narrator's claim. The narrator's sense of being assailed by the forces of history is unsurprising given the way the domestic dramas of the family replay the injustices inflicted upon the Japanese Canadian community during the Second World War. The family's move from British Columbia to the interior of Alberta, while not a consequence of the Japanese Canadian internment, mirrors that historical forced migration. The oppressive terms of these relocations are conveyed through the experiences of the sisters. Finding themselves stuck on an unwelcoming plot of land in the unrelentingly stifling heat, the girls are unable even to complain about the situation. Instead, they choke back their unhappiness and force themselves to eat the fried chicken their father has brought back from town. The allegorical implications of the narrator's concerted efforts to swallow the distasteful drumsticks, the "two disgusting legs, the gristly white threads growing like tapeworms in [her] stomach," without crying openly before her family members are clear for the many Japanese Canadians who quietly endured the internment (36).[1]

The historical internment is explicitly invoked as a key intertext during a conversation between the father and the local motel owner shortly after the family arrived in their new hometown. The tense exchange between these men underlines the complicated politics of arrival that mark the family's location within rural Alberta, as well as how Asian communities are more broadly situated within the dominant narrative of national identity. The motel owner, in an attempt to be hospitable, expresses his disagreement with the government's internment policies but is rebuffed by the father's loud anger:

> "I always thought it was terrible what was done to you people."

> Which ones? I thought. Which ones does he think we are?
> "What you say?" Dad took a quick step toward the gulping man.
> Okasan raised one hand but it dropped heavily beside her body.
> "No offense intended," Motel Man stammered. "I figured you folks to be Japanese."
> "We are CANADIAN!" Dad roared.
> "No need," Okasan nervously plucked Dad's sleeve. "No need to shout," she murmured.
> Swinging arc of arm. Smack. A hand-shaped stain on my mother's cheek, the color of pain and humiliation. (70)

The father's violent response, spurred on by the motel owner's liberal sympathies but received by the mother, is clearly a rejection of a narrative of Canadian identity that excludes racialized bodies. It is, after all, precisely this sentiment that enabled the government to carry out and profit from its devastating internment policies. But in this dismissal of the motel owner's comment for interpellating the family as Japanese rather than Canadian, the father also utterly refuses to be read through the historical lens of Japanese Canadian struggles. By prohibiting this conversation, the father effectively shuts down discussions about the legacies of institutionalized practices of discrimination aimed at Japanese Canadians and other racialized bodies, and refuses to acknowledge the troubling terrain the contemporary moment is perched upon. In this way, the father's lashing out at the mother as a response to his dissatisfaction with liberal sentiments warns us of the dangers of ignoring history.

The father's attempts to cultivate the family's plot of land in Alberta with rice further underscores the perils of neglecting history.[2] The narrator and her sisters are forced to steal water from their neighbours to feed their father's "rice-growing obsession," a task that takes a toll on their bodies and psyches (197). By refusing to acknowledge the arid reality of the Albertan landscape, the father constructs it as both inhospitable and a space to be conquered. While tilling the land much like an indentured labourer, the narrator recognizes that long ago, "the prairie was just an ancient ocean" (181). She is, however, alone in her epiphany as her father reasserts his efforts to colonize the land through the migrant labour of his family and to realize his vision of the present moment. The seemingly arbitrary nature of this aspiration, when coupled with the merciless implementation of the plan, translates into despair for the children:

> No one knew what compelled our father to try and grow Japanese rice in Alberta. No one knew what we were doing in boxcars disguised as a motel.
>
> No one knew how long we had to stay there. No one knew. What we did know was that no one would save us. (114)

And it is this unremitting despair that threatens to be the most overwhelming of all forces.

One of the narrator's few saving graces during her childhood is her friendship with a neighbour, Gerald Nakamura Coming Singer, who lives with his Japanese Canadian mother, Janice. Despite the pleasure she feels with Gerald's company, the narrator finds herself hurling cruel words at her friend after a particularly grueling episode of digging to steal the Snyders' water. Gerald appears on the scene just as the narrator is feeling despondent over her lack of escape routes. She realizes that "[g]oing to white outsiders wasn't an option for an Asian immigrant family like us. If you ditched the family, there was absolutely nothing left. When you are ten, something is better than nothing, even if something has a hand faster than the words forming in your head, let alone in your mouth" (199). In a scene that strongly resembles the earlier episode between the father and the motel owner, Gerald's offering of compassion and comfort is rejected as the narrator feels a "hateful coil of ugliness twisting in my gut, the words stinging something inside me, but unable to stop" (200). Upon ending this friendship, the narrator is met with words of praise from her father: "'Good for you,' my father nodded approvingly. 'Shouldn't be friends with weaklings'" (201). Responding to her frustration with many things, including a recognition of how her father's impossible dreams have distorted both his humanity and hers, the narrator turns her face up to "[t]he fat sun rising keen and relentless, [and howls] until [her] mouth was parched and cracked" (201). Her despair, which cannot be articulated through conventional speech or through familiar narratives, understandably leaves her father feeling quite confused.

This painful episode with Gerald, however, is not the only occasion in which the narrator finds herself emulating her father. The narrator describes her complicated relationship with her father and states in a moment of honest vulnerability that "[i]t isn't like *I* feel an overwhelming surge of affection whenever I think of our father, but, I don't know, an emotion I can't name stays small and silent in the depths of my heart. I can't cut off my feelings from him, my monster, my hero" (245). And, earlier in the novel, when she is exhausted after long shifts at work, the narrator thinks that she may need a new vehicle "[l]ike my dad['s]!" (184) This transmission of violence and despair between generations makes the task of reconciling with historical injustices incredibly difficult. As an adult, the narrator returns to the childhood home and demands reparation from her father for the pain he has caused her sisters, her mother, and herself. After literally choking an apology out of him, she is shocked by her own actions and forced to admit that what she longs for, "[s]omething that will erase the past, right all wrongs, so we can be whole creatures again," does not exist (260). Indeed, any resolution that seeks to place the entire burden upon the father without implicating the narrator is perhaps as impossible a fantasy as the Albertan rice fields.

The book begins by implicating the narrator within a neocolonial landscape littered with signs of commodity culture. Indeed, she introduces herself to the reader in the first line of the text by stating that "I am a collector of abandoned shopping carts" (9). By profession, the narrator is one who collects debris from the urban landscape and reclaims that which has been discarded and forgotten. And yet, despite her function as one who reintegrates neglected elements of capitalist culture, recycling past products into the present, she tells us that once she has realized it is Easter and therefore time for the family reunion, she would "rather go on collecting the lost carts than make the pilgrimage home" (10). The marked preference for inhabiting her current role as an extension of commodity culture in the contemporary moment instead of returning to the difficult landscape of parental homes and histories speaks to the ongoing work of colonial conquest. The connection between past and present activities and the troubling positions of father and daughter are made explicit in an early description of the holiday: "This weekend is a long one, and the business shuffle turned into a mass exodus for the markets. Instead of bidding for pipes, steel cables, real estate, and crude oil, human suits are clamoring in long lineups for carcasses of meat, fowl, and the limbs of large mammals" (9). This passage then renders visible the doubled meaning of the word "occupation," as both profession and colonization of land, and the interconnections that run through this novel. Any return to the past implicitly requires a consideration of the spatial dimensions of that existence and the problems of occupation, positioning, and territory—and, in this way, ultimately asks for a consideration of the contiguous and often overlapping existences of Asian diasporic and First Nations communities in Canada.

Contiguous Tricksters

Toward the end of the narrative, the narrator finds herself off duty and driving through the downtown area of Calgary. It is a moment of desolation, both in terms of the cityscape and the narrator's emotional state. She looks at the empty urban core and thinks,

> Abandoned, I can imagine a post-apocalyptic world of crumbling concrete, the struggle for clean water. Or maybe, when humans are gone, our myths will come alive, wander over the remnants of our uncivilization. Kappa, water dragons, yamauba, oni. Selkie, golem, lorelei, xuan wu. The creatures we carry will be born from our demise and the world will dream a new existence. (223)

Hers is a vision that disrupts conventional understandings of the present as civilized. She dreams instead of a future born from the bowels of the contemporary moment in which global mythologies are able to coexist. This simultaneously utopic and dystopic vision suggests that cultural stories may be able to teach us how to construct more hospitable futures. At the same time, this postapocalyptic vision also asks us to consider how such stories and those who tell them are located within landscapes.

As a child, the narrator remembers one year when her father was actually successful in his rice-growing endeavour. For once, the prairies received an abundance of rain and the rice flourished, a spectacle their neighbour Janice called an "unnatural sight" (227). It is also the same summer that the narrator spotted kappa footprints in the muddy rice fields. The footprints suggest that "a gleeful creature had ran jubilantly over every inch of the amazing wetness, jumping, leaping, dancing, stepping exquisite toes, perfectly webbed," and this sense of joy spreads to both the narrator's father and mother when they behold the marks (228). Upon seeing the traces of the kappa, the father becomes visibly softer and more human, but also wonders to himself, "But how?" he murmured, "in this country, this climate? Where would it have come from? Emigrated like us?" (229). The question of how a Japanese kappa comes to exist in Blackfoot territory, southeast of Lethbridge, somewhere between the Oldman River and the Milk River, is never resolved for the father, and the possibility that it, like the family, might have emigrated is never one that he entertains seriously. The aridity of the prairies suggests that the Albertan landscape would be hostile for the kappa, given its distinctive dependency on water. The narrator describes the difficulty of obtaining water for the rice fields in other years because the two closest rivers are still both distant and inadequate sources, with "Old Man River flowing sluggish brown north of us and the Milk River, chocolate, winding too far south" (126). And yet, the kappa clearly is able to exist and bestow good fortune in this Canadian landscape.

Perhaps, then, the more pressing question raised by the kappa is not, as the father asks, how did it arrive here, but instead, how does it manage to flourish while others like his family struggle to exist. The answer seems to lie in the relationship that each has to the local space. When the narrator comments on the coincidence of the successful rice crop and the sighting of the kappa that year, she contemplates the possibility that

> Okasan's and Dad's good-luck kappa must have left some green goodness behind, despite all my pooh-poohing and cynical comments. We had an incredible crop, handpicked in the old-fashioned way, and each grain so sweet it flooded our mouths with juicy longing.
>
> Dad's one and only ever rice crop. Something he wouldn't get over for the rest of his life.
>
> But we were thankful, that year, that summer, and at Christmas, I received a diving watch that could withstand water pressure up to fifty meters. Me inwardly snorting, when the hell had I ever gone diving? Where would I go that was fifty meters deep? Milk Chocolate River perhaps? The Old Man?

> But I was touched, all the same, and wore the gift constantly. Sending thanks to a questionable creature from a different clime. A creature much greener than Santa. (231)

Throughout the text, the narrator constantly meanders through Blackfoot territory, but fails to recognize it as such. For instance, she refers repeatedly to Naapi, the Old Man, without ever realizing that the river's name comes from Blackfoot legends about this land. The difference between the kappa and Santa/Naapi is described in terms of degrees of greenness rather than as absolute difference, but the narrator never seems to realize fully the implications of her insight.[3] And while Gerald's narrative echoes and overlaps with the narrator's in multiple and interesting ways, especially given his own displacement once his parents part ways, these intersections completely elude the narrator's attention. When Gerald's father decides to return to the Blood reserve, Gerald is left in limbo. His mother Janice notes that "Gerald didn't want to go with him and he didn't want to stay with me. So now's all he got is attitude" (163). Given the timeline of the novel, it is likely that Gerald would be without Native status and therefore unable, even if he had wanted, to accompany his father to the reserve.[4] Gerald's eventual relocation to Vancouver to live with his aunt reverses the migration pattern of the narrator while remaining shaped by the paternalistic authority of the Canadian government.

Fixated on surviving her own childhood, the narrator's unhappiness prevents her from seeing the rich history of the Albertan space around her and from making connections with others. By explicitly linking the family's move to the prairies with the Japanese Canadian internment, the novel implicitly draws upon the dominant perception of the interior as empty land, filled only with abandoned mining and other ghost towns. The language of national security mobilized by the government during the Second World War becomes a way of allowing the government to appropriate property and strip people of their citizenship rights while also forcing Japanese Canadians to participate in the colonial myth of unoccupied territory. The relocation is perceived as emptying the west coast of Japanese Canadians to protect the nation, all without inconveniencing anyone else. Thus, when the narrator as a ten-year-old child takes her shovel to the land in order to try to produce the rice paddies her father demands, she engages in a violent relationship with the land, but this repetition is more complicated than previous settlement narratives that deliberately neglected Indigenous presences. The narrator's participation within this framework is clearly coerced, but this factor does not make her speech or actions any less damaging in either the past or present tense. The transplantation of the rice, with the exception of that one year when it flourishes, represents an impossible set of cultural relations that operate through imposition and ahistoricism, and that radically differ from those embodied by the kappa. The migration of the Japanese kappa then gives us a way of imagining harmonious coexistences that do not resort to strategies of colonial violence. The kappa's ability to live alongside Blackfoot tricksters without claiming the social imagination in absolute terms opens up ways of reading the intersecting narratives of Japanese Canadian internment, the family's relocation to the prairies, and the ongoing displacement of the indigenous inhabitants.

Cultural Baggage

Intersecting with these traumatic childhood memories and descriptions of collecting shopping carts are the narrator's intimate encounters with a mysterious Stranger. She describes the Stranger she meets at a wedding banquet in Chinatown as "beautiful beyond belief" at first and then later, upon closer scrutiny, as having "an oddly shaped head, strands of thin hair hanging long and limp. . . . In the strange glow of the streetlight, the Stranger's complexion looked almost olive" (85). These shifting appearances are initially easily explained as the result of distance and lighting, but take on increasing significance when the Stranger's appearance shifts again. The narrator and the Stranger head to the tarmac of the Calgary airport to watch the lunar eclipse, but find themselves wrestling Japanese-style. When disrobing, a necessary prerequisite according to the Stranger, the narrator realizes that "the Stranger looked almost greenish, skin hairless and moist" (122). As the Stranger turns to face the narrator, she says she "could only gaze with wonder. No nipples. Nor a bellybutton" (122). This sumo tori, intensely physical contact, has significant consequences for the narrator. When she manages to wrestle the

Stranger to the ground and accidentally knocks off her hat to reveal "a strangely shaped head," the narrator describes how "something cool-wet spilled, covered me in a liquid sweetness. I thought she came. Came in waves of pleasure" (124). The outcomes of this extensive and physical contact are not ones that the narrator could have imagined or is able to explain. She believes that this act has impregnated her, despite realizing how such a condition would contradict the fundamentals of human biology. The description of the Stranger as green, with a bowl-shaped head filled with water, and as able to shift forms, makes it clear that the narrator's wrestling partner is a kappa. Although the narrator's sense of being literally pregnant is never completely confirmed or refuted, the text also introduces a metaphorical reading of her condition. The splash of liquid that the narrator interprets as an orgasm is also the source of life for the kappa. Without it, the consequences are unbearable:

> *And when kappa despair, when their green skin grows dry and brittle, when kappa eyes succumb to pain, when kappa parents turn aside their kappa children, when kappa deny water, they rip the tender skin from between their fingers and toes. They rip their water bowl from atop their noble heads. They tear off their turtle shells and expose their flesh to the sun. They turn their eyes away from all things kappa.*
>
> *They become humans.* (176, emphasis in original)

The kappa's willingness to have her water bowl spilled allows for a moment of intense vulnerability and intimacy. The life that the narrator then feels growing inside her can also be read as the planting of hope. The encounters with the kappa serve to educate the narrator about the connections between pleasure, intimacy, and regeneration.

But the kappa's lessons are neither simple nor easy to learn, and this difficulty is illustrated by an exchange between the kappa and the narrator that occurs toward the end of the novel. After stumbling upon two of her sisters having lunch together, the narrator sits down with them and is surprised by who her sisters have become. She realizes that each of her sisters, Slither, PG, and Mice, have grown out of their childhood selves and are no longer people with whom she is familiar. Her ongoing worries about PG's safety, the narrator thinks to herself, have been "nothing but the reflections of my own sorry circumstances and I really need a kick in the butt" (245). This epiphany highlights how much more self-aware the narrator has become. Slither's gift of a beautician's business card leaves the narrator feeling "[e]xasperated, annoyed, and also touched for her way of expressing concern," a response that is markedly different from her earlier angry reactions (246). This increasing willingness to accept her sister's affections are encouraged by the kappa, who suddenly reappears in the restaurant's washroom after a prolonged absence in the narrator's life. Instead of beginning by discussing the narrator's pregnancy, for which the kappa is somehow partially responsible, the kappa encourages the narrator to visit the hairstylist, stating, "We don't come from a Samsonite culture" (247). The narrator responds by retorting, "That's a suitcase company!" (247). Without providing any significant insight into the narrator's possibly pregnant condition, but extolling the pleasures of visiting a barbershop, the kappa then vanishes.

I find this exchange between the narrator and the kappa significant for the misreading that the narrator commits, and also for the misreading that she does not commit. The narrator finds the kappa's comment ludicrous because her immediate referent for "Samsonite" is the Japanese luggage maker. In this way, she implies that the company's description of its corporate vision to "transform itself into a leading global lifestyle travel company," and presumably to become synonymous with travel, has achieved a level of success that surely surpasses even the corporation's initial hopes. The kappa's intention seems to have been to invoke the Christian story of Samson's betrayal by his lover Delilah and the subsequent loss of his strength when his hair was shorn. Although there are potentially interesting ways of interpreting that missed reference, I am more intrigued by a third layer of meaning that is overlooked. Despite the multiple lawsuits filed in Alberta by various Cree bands (including the Samson Cree, whose claims were worth billions of dollars) during the late 1980s and early 1990s, a period of much legal action that intersects with the timeline of this novel, the narrator does not make the connection between the kappa's words and the land claims.[5] The narrator's instinctive association of "Samsonite" with the corporation suggests that her narrative, a *Bildungsroman* of sorts, is nestled between at least two other epistemological frameworks. That she does not catch the Biblical allusion might imply a certain shift away from the settler ideology that she had embraced earlier (a connection made explicit through her childhood obsession with Laura Ingalls and *Little House on the Prairie*), but the narrator's inability to connect the term to the ongoing land claims, even if only to later reject the link as a misreading, suggests that it is not easy to unlearn colonial ideologies. This (mis)understanding occurs toward the end of the text rather than the beginning, which underscores the impossibility of reading Goto's novel as a successful novel of kappa education. The narrator's understanding of the Samsonite reference then becomes a moment that directs the reader's attention to the difficulties of working through one's cultural baggage in all the senses of that term.

The kappa's response to the narrator's dismissive comment, "We don't come from a Samsonite culture," is to state, "You're not listening" (247). The narrator's sense of being overwhelmed by her own pain and complicated family history leaves her wondering, "When do memories lose their power? There must be an expiry date. Maybe PG's choice of physical distance isn't such a bad idea. Maybe PG's family baggage is still in heaps in the downstairs bedroom, cluttering the floor until Okasan finally boxes it up" (171). Instead of connecting to others who also feel hurt by their realities, the narrator's experiences serve to isolate her from the larger social world. This Samsonite exchange, then, has significant implications, given that the narrator's inability to listen, a condition diagnosed by the kappa, occurs precisely at the moment when the narrator is the most receptive that she has ever been throughout the entire text. If, after all of this work that has been undertaken by the kappa, the narrator, and her sisters, she still cannot hear, then what possibilities exist for undoing colonial violence?

The novel reminds us that there are differences between the narrator and her father, and that it is possible to work toward the closing of past injuries once the extent of those wounds is understood. Historical pain, in this novel, is experienced by all parties; the father is certainly not exempt. His nostalgic efforts to grow rice—"All he knew was that we needed water to make the flooded soft mud of his childhood thought-place, years disremembered and half a world away"—speak to a sense of urban dislocation as an adult in Japan as well as to displacement in rural Alberta (126-7). It is, however, his desire to create a past long gone without being conscious of the price extorted from those in the present moment that translates into material and symbolic violence. Consequently, the narrator is left burdened by historical pain, but she is also given an opportunity to address these fractured narratives. Her friendship with Gerald introduces dialogue between Asian Canadian and Indigenous communities and, as the narrator's description of her first visit to Gerald's home makes clear, the challenges of entering into this conversation:

> Gerald Nakamura Coming Singer was incomprehensible. In Laura Ingalls' book-world, Indians meant teepees on the prairies and that was that. Indians didn't equal someone who was both Blood and Japanese-Canadian. Indians certainly never meant someone who lived next door on a chicken farm.
>
> "Call me Janice," she croaked and thumped me on my arm, when I called Gerald's mom, Mrs Nakamura Coming Singer.
>
> I eye-glanced at Gerald's face for signs. Flipping from his face to his mother's, searching for where the ancestry bled into more Japanese and less Indian, but I couldn't tell, and only stared with my pea-sized eyes until Janice noticed.
>
> "Whatchya staring at, kiddo? You never seen a First Nations person before?"
>
> "First Nations?"
>
> "Yeah, kiddo. Don't cut me any of the 'Indian' crap, how they keep teaching that shit in school, I'll never understand!" (188-9)

The narrator reflects upon this exchange and tells us that when she had first moved east, "I didn't really think about Indians, First Nations or otherwise. I didn't really think" (189). Although the blossoming friendship with Gerald becomes an opportunity to rectify this gap in her thinking, it causes her to feel guilty and apprehensive. When Gerald and the narrator speak on the telephone as adults, he tells her that he has long since forgiven her for those terrible comments she made as a child. And yet, when he invites her to visit him on his mother's farm, she waffles, afraid to take him up on his offer even though her heart yells, "Go see him!" (240) This hesitation is, however, a sign of the important distinction between the narrator and her father, since it comes out of her desire to handle this relationship with care.

Water

The novel ends with the narrator in the company of her friends and a new romantic interest. Having driven outside of the city limits to watch a planetary conjunction, the characters look up and, although they are unable to see the planets, they are greeted by an unexpected rain shower. Surprised by the precipitation, the narrator and her companions embrace this new turn of events by leaping into the rain:

> We hold out palms to catch the wet in the cups of our hands, tip our heads, drink from the skies. . . . Soaring, we leap skyward, leave perfect footprints in the rich mud. New green shoots of life twine at our feet, rising leafy in the warm night air. And in the collage of green, the movements of our bodies, I can see kappa rising from the soil, like creatures waking from enforced hibernation, they stretch their long, green limbs with gleeful abandon. Skin moist, wet, slick and salamander-soft, kappa and humans dance together, our lives unfurling before us.
>
> And the water breaks free with the rain. (275)

This depiction of the women revelling in the rain is a clear moment of hope and a sign of the kappa's effectiveness. This link between the kappa and the narrator's present joy are further underscored when the narrator picks up her new girlfriend, Bernie, and feels "a flow of sweet liquid fil[l] [her] . . . veins" (272). Although this representation is unarguably an optimistic one, it occurs on the penultimate page of the text. The final pages of the novel are instead filled by an invitation that reads, "*I am a creature of the water. / I am a kappa child. / Come, embrace me*" (276). And after that, the text provides the reader with a glossary of kappa-related terms and pertinent history, and then finally the author's acknowledgements.

Reading this ending, which unfurls for a few pages, eventually meandering toward a conclusion, is quite suggestive given the kinds of discussions this novel makes possible. Although I realize that the positioning of the author's acknowledgements at the end of the text may simply be the result of the publisher's preferences, I nonetheless think they suggest a way of moving outside of the text in a way that foregrounds acknowledging support and friendship while also heeding the effects of neglect and violence. The rolling ending of this text then moves between the ideas of pleasure and transformation invoked by the image of the women in the rain to the world outside of this narrative, all the while encouraging the reader to heed the kappa's call for sustained pleasure and intimacy. The glossary suggests ways in which the kappa exists outside of the pages of the novel in the space of cultural mythology as well as in the everyday world, having been sighted "on mainland Asia" (277). The glossary reminds us again that the kappa "lives in the borders between natural and human environments . . . [and] can be beaten only by spilling the water from its bowlshaped head," reiterating the interdependent nature of survival, risk, and intimacy (277).

Goto's novel as a whole, but especially its conclusion, assumes a new and particularly urgent set of meanings for me as a reader newly located on the west coast of Canada. The glossary reiterates ways to defeat the kappa in what is really the final page of the novel proper and therefore the novel's, if not the text's, final words. These instructions about emptying the kappa's water bowl resonate in particularly discomforting ways given the ongoing efforts to privatize water in British Columbia. Given that this novel stresses the symbolic significance of water for a Japanese Canadian community more specifically, but also for Asian diasporic communities more broadly, larger questions about the responsibilities of diasporic communities to public resources are raised. The dereliction of these duties results in both enormous ethical and cultural dilemmas given the vision the kappa puts forward. Moreover, this current debate over water as a potentially private resource asks us to consider how we, just like Goto's narrator, occupy particular positions within this same public.

It is, of course, a plight that echoes the narrator's crime of stealing water from her neighbours. Although hers is a fictionalized account, the consequences are still worth considering for their relevance to this current and very real-life situation. While taking a break from stealing water for her father's impossible rice paddy, the narrator looks for the first time at the landscape:

> The stars were loud. They buzzed with light and the summer breeze cooled the sweat along my hairline. Only then did I

> notice the sweet sound of the crickets. Breathed in the fresh scent of corn ripening into peaches and cream, summer grass turning into hay.
>
> How beautiful it could be, I thought, and trembled I don't know why. I plunked down in the sea turned desert, lay in brittle grass. Huge, shiny crickets crawled across my body, paused and played their songs before passing. I stared at the incredible sky, rich, dense, almost dizzying. The stars quivered. (199)

This moment produces a recognition of the double bind in which she is caught. The narrator perceives fully the futility of her father's efforts to recreate Japan in Alberta and feels immense shame at being forced to undertake this theft of resources. At the same time, she is also bound to her despotic father by love, kinship, and a recognition of their similarities. Her ensuing callous treatment of Gerald occurs at this point in the novel, and after she realizes her very limited options. The decision to survive by lashing out with cruelty comes at the cost of her humanity, as she is consequently unable to appreciate falling stars or feel desire. The attempt to resume this friendship is never fully actualized and indeed cannot be until the narrator can be sure that she is capable of true friendship. Although the narrator never reaches that point and never fully relinquishes the past narratives that have shaped her, she strives toward a more hopeful future. Her sister Satomi tells her that "[i]f you don't let the hatred go, he continues to oppress your life, just like if you were still living in his house" (266). Although the narrator accepts this advice, she is deeply entangled within narratives that refuse easy solutions.

The father's theft of water is motivated by nostalgia, a desire to remake the land into home, and a fear of surviving outside of this narrative. *The Kappa Child* gives us a complicated representation of this paternal figure, complete with insight into how he came to personify such violence and how it damaged his children and wife. Before moving to Canada, he was a husband that Okasan's friends admired because he was a teetotaler. It is only after the family migrates that the father is transformed into a monstrous figure addicted to nasal spray. The narrator speculates that somehow the aridity of the interior "filled my father's head so mucus-full he couldn't breathe without it. Nasal spray. His cavities filled with memories lost, or maybe the unattainable future" (126).

Even if this explanation of her father's frustrations does not justify his actions, it does suggest a diasporic relationship to both a public and its communal resources that requires both self-criticality and compassion.

Reading this novel in the contemporary moment invites pressing questions about how to reconcile the failed dreams of diaspora with the violences they have helped enact, and about the possibilities for forging new narratives not laden with guilt but still mindful of the past. The goal of thinking through these kinds of questions is not to stuff our Samsonite luggage with more liberal guilt or reach easy milktoast answers, but to think about our contiguous existences that often overlap in challenging ways. These various trickster figures, whether Indigenous or diasporic, operate as provocations to thinking, acting, and being. As ethical and political guides that intersect in many ways, one visible instance being that of water, these tricksters give us a means of thinking through potential conversations around specific common issues and suggest ways of moving in new directions. Through its use of the trickster figure, *The Kappa Child* reminds us of the importance of curiosity and the need to make space for it in the world. The kappa's curiosity gets it into difficulties, but these dilemmas more often than not become situations of learning. The kappa's willingness to explore opens up new possibilities for readers, but also lets us remain conscious of the shaping forces of culture, history, and geography. For Asian diasporas, one of the lessons the kappa tries to teach is the need to participate in new conversations that are not necessarily spaces of safety, but ask us to reckon constantly with the unknown in risky ways.

This is an updated and revised version of "Diasporic Violences, Uneasy Friendships, and The Kappa Child,*" previously published in* Troubling Tricksters: Revisioning Critical Conversations, *edited by Deanna Reder and Linda M. Morra, Wilfrid Laurier University Press, 2010.*

AUSTIN CLARKE

Austin Clarke's Poetic Turn

Leslie Sanders

> Where poetry is liberative language, connecting the fragments within us, connecting us to others like and unlike ourselves, replenishing our desire. . . . In poetry words can say more than they mean and mean more than they say. In a time of frontal assaults both on language and on human solidarity, poetry can remind us of all we are in danger of losing—disturb us, embolden us out of resignation.
>
> ADRIENNE RICH

Author of eleven novels, eight short-story collections, and six memoirs of varying length, Canadian Barbadian Austin Clarke nonetheless frequently insisted that he really wanted to be a poet. He told the novelist H Nigel Thomas that he began with poetry, while still in Barbados, and boasted of winning a poetry prize in his first year at Trinity College, University of Toronto; he included the winning poem, and one other, in his midcareer *The Austin Clarke Reader* (Thomas 2006, 33). His biographer Stella Algoo-Baksh reports that Clarke continued to experiment with poetry in the early 1960s (Algoo-Baksh 1994, 45). Yet it was only in his last few years that Clarke turned to poetry in earnest. The result: two long poems, *Where the Sun Shines Best* (2013) and *In Your Crib* (2015), both published by Guernica Editions, accomplishments in which he took inordinate pleasure.[1]

This essay asks: why the turn to poetry after a life in fiction? What did poetry allow Austin Clarke to do that prose did not? The poet and novelist Dionne Brand provides a way to consider these questions that is both richly suggestive and incisive. In an unpublished article, "An Ars Poetica from the Blue Clerk," Brand meditates more generally on the matter of poetry and prose for Black writers, and proposes poetry as a diacritic for narratives of Black life. She writes:

> Much in the way that diacritical marks supplement certain alphabets, changing the sound, tone, or meaning of certain words, poetry, in my formulation, changes what I see as the racist alphabets of narratives—the prevalent modes of speech and key impediments to black being. I am proposing a radical indictment of "narrative." I think that for Black people, narrative, as it is constituted now, is incapable of transmitting or sounding a tomorrow, beyond brutalization. It is incapable of transmitting or sounding a present, a today, since our lived today is cluttered in frequencies of oppression and responses to oppression. In the presence of our bodies all narrative utterances are full of attention to racism, bracketed by racism, animated by racism; our language is noded, mined, secretly and publicly by racism. Self-reference, self-description, are circumscribed by the mined terrain of narrative.

Using Christina Sharpe's concept of "dysgraphia," that is, the ways in which continual media representations insist upon "Black social, material and psychic death," Brand describes narrative as

> almost always implicated in the colonial/imperialist/racist project—with best efforts one writes back to, or against, first the existence and then the persistence of the dominant narratives of coloniality, racism and imperialism. Character in narrative, in this sense, and landscape for that matter, are weighted with "whiteness" as a fundamental/originary category. The black body in narrative is always spectacular, always spectacularised, marked. The dysgraphia, of dominant and of dominating narratives, unwrites, and makes incoherent, black presence as presence.

Poetry, Brand speculates, offers "a way to dislodge a fixity of meaning, as critique of and a remedy/cure for the fragmented black body of narrative."

In her indictment of narrative, Brand throws into bold relief the strictures and constraints produced by the need always to write against, to resist what is overdetermined by the landscape and meanings of the dominant imaginary. Clarke's fiction perfectly illustrates her characterizations of narrative, and is deeply illuminated by them. His turn to poetry indeed provides him respite from the confines of his narratives, and freedom to consider and express what they do not permit.

Austin Clarke is well known and deeply appreciated for the ways in which his novels and short stories, written over half a century, dramatize the lives of Caribbean immigrants to Canada, both their experiences and those of their children, or more precisely, their sons. All Clarke's Toronto-based fictions insist upon the inhospitableness of white Canadian society, its refusal to accord a space in which black life might flourish. Thus, in spite of the fact that some of his characters, for example, Boysie, in the third book of his Toronto trilogy,[2] *The Bigger Light* (1975), the nameless protagonist of *The Question* (1999), and Tim and John of *The Origin of Waves* (1997) have achieved material success, their sense of self remains vulnerable, constantly defined and endangered by the racist script that Canadian racial attitudes impose. Clarke's insistent illumination of that script simultaneously discloses the suffering and unbelonging of his community and gives lie to white Canadian insistent self-regard as embracing multiculturalism and as superior to its southern neighbour. Pointedly, police murder of black men punctuates Clarke's fiction, concluding his most recent novel, *More*, but depicted or a topic of conversation in earlier work as well.

In *Blackening Canada* (2015), Paul Barrett argues that psychic and literal immobility pervades the narratives, and the characters, of Clarke's later fiction. For example, he writes,

> In "Sometimes, A Motherless Child," Clarke depicts young black masculinity in Canada by contrasting the chronotope of the automobile with the immobility of the space of the jail cell. In his depiction of young and older black men, Clarke reveals how the longing for social mobility is expressed in black men's physical movement and is circumvented by the criminalization of black masculinity (70).

Working with Franz Fanon's depiction of the colonial subject, Barrett continues:

> Fanon's colonial subject might dream of a violent ending to the colony that will restore his psychic and social mobility, but such an escape from immobility is impossible for Clarke's characters. Clarke's work shows how the spaces of the bar, the police station, and the government office are as immobilizing for Clarke's diasporic characters as they are for Fanon's colonial subject. (71)

In some respects, this immobility describes Clarke's earlier work as well. For example, "The Motor Car," in the collection *When He Was Free and Young and He Used to Wear Silks* (1971), similarly depicts a young man's joy in the mobility his car affords him. In that early story, through a quick-witted change of costume and pose, Calvin escapes detection as the cause of the accident that kills the Canadian girl he invited to ride with him, and apparently goes on his way; however, the story's opening sentence suggests that accountability lies in his future: "That Canadian thing you see lying down there in that bed is Calvin woman, I mean *was* Calvin woman" (90).

In these early stories, and in the Toronto trilogy, the narratives bespeak a newness to Canada, finding it alien, as much as hostile. The astonishment or naiveté of many of his characters concerning the racist practices of their new environment in the early works, however, soon gives way to a bitter understanding of racism's intractability. For example, in *The Question* and *The Origin of Waves*, the principal characters are older, further into their Canadian lives, and while we rarely are told their occupation their relations to place, even though settled, remain wary and ambivalent. After almost half a century, Clarke's narratives suggest, the landscape remains the same; only it is, to the characters, more legible.

What has changed is Clarke's generational perspective. In *More*, for example, Clarke portrays black youth as part of the fabric of the city. However, they speak a language those around them do not understand. Idora's son, BJ, has become a Muslim, and portraits of Garvey, Cleaver, Coltrane, and Malcolm cover the walls of his room, to her bewilderment. The BJ we meet in "Sometimes a Motherless Child" (an earlier version of this aspect of *More*) also is a voracious reader; however, in that short story, we are told what he does, and we know that the police killed him. In *More*, his activities are not disclosed. A conversation among some youth overheard by Idora on the subway suggests that they are targeting her son and have some involvement with him. Finally, at the conclusion of that novel, it is not clear whether they or the police have killed BJ. The world BJ navigates is even more perilous than that his elders had to negotiate.

Despite the hostile world Clarke's characters inhabit, his fiction is ambivalent about direct resistance. In "The Motor Car," Calvin fumes about a friend in Barbados who asks him for money, signing his letter Willy X: " . . . he sure now that Willy gone mad too, like everybody else he been reading bout in the States and in England; black people gone mad, Calvin say . . . all this damn foolishness bout Power to the People . . . " (101). In the main, this sentiment describes the view of his first-generation characters, who are preoccupied by what their Canadian context makes impossible, or inexpressible, not with how they might fight for change. Only in *The Polished Hoe* (2002), set in midtwentieth century Barbados, does revenge for injustice occur. That much-acclaimed novel comprises the night-long confession by Mary-Matilde of her murder of the plantation owner to whom she was "mistress," and who was both her father and father of her child.[3]

Clarke's fiction, then, both depicts and expresses the social, political, and psychic landscape of Caribbean immigrants, their inner turmoil and psychic damage, as well as their vision and experience of Canadian society. Often a first-person persona or an individual consciousness comprises the narrative voice in his short stories, this device producing a point of view that is both intense and confining, insisting upon ways in which the central character's life is constrained. Expansion in these stories, as in other Clarke work, is a matter of memory. In his essay "'Voices Under the Window' of Representation: Austin Clarke's Poetics of (Body)-Memory in *The Meeting Point*," Michael Bucknor accounts for Clarke's narrative style, filled with ruptures, tangents, ellipses, asides, as typically triggered by what he calls "body-memory"; he quotes Clarke's comment to Terrance Craig that he "tries to have the story go forward not on one plane but on several planes, and the injection into the narrative of the thinking of the man" (Bucknor 2013, 186). Bucknor's concept of body-memory, then, unfolds the meaning and methods of Clarke's departure from "realism" and the strictures of a literal representation. However, at times when the narrative voice is first-person, an effect of this technique is a paradoxical depth and narrowness of vision. The horizons in much of Clarke's fiction are narrow as a result, a narrowness his poetry escapes.

In his poetry, Clarke is free of many of the strictures that his prose imposes, both stylistically and, I will argue, emotionally. Reviewers have described the poetry as continuing the concerns of Clarke's fiction and other prose. They are not incorrect in doing so; however, expecting those similarities, they miss important differences.

The long poem *Where the Sun Shines Best* was provoked by and responds to the brutal murder of a homeless man, Paul Crouch, in 2005. The murder, committed by three army reservists, took place in Moss Park, which was across the street from Clarke's home. *Where the Sun Shines Best* comprises an act of witnessing that is unique in Clarke's corpus in several respects. Of the brutalities and losses recounted in Clarke's Toronto-based fiction, none describe physical violence directly, and none concern a white victim. In fact, in his short story "If the Bough Breaks," a group of women at the hairdressers witness the rough arrest, guns drawn, of a young girl who is white and univocally refuse her sympathy until, later in the story, it transpires that their hairdresser knows her, and that the police have raped and beaten her, and then returned her to the site of the arrest. United by gender, and an understanding of the experience of violation, it is her violation that elicits their sympathy, despite her race.

The literal landscape of *Where the Sun Shines Best* is Moss Park, a downtown park surrounded by public housing, and also town houses, which the poem describes as "patterned / after England, Victorian and Georgian; their windows sealed / against the cold draught of the night . . . intolerant of the blackness outside" (27). The poet aside, these residents never venture into the park. Its denizens by day are Muslim women with their strollers, by night homeless people, alcoholics, and prostitutes. The poet's vision of the inhabitants is, he acknowledges, partially obscured; he remarks, regarding one man, "His head is cut off, beheaded suddenly / by my window that is too small to frame his shoulders" (12). The opening stanza declares the poem's concerns:

> The yellow leaves are trampled over by the black
> boots of three soldiers from the Moss Park Armouries;
> in uniform, intended not to be seen, or identified
> for their intention and profession is to kill
> to shoot from a distance, clean and perfect
> and wipe their minds clean, erase all imperfection
> of marksmanship. War. War has been declared.
> War. It is all that's on their minds. War;
> and the intention for war declared upon Moss Park.

Balancing the three reservists, Clarke introduces a mute chorus: " . . . three other men standing as if at attention, / though they are no soldiers; one man's posture is stooped / with old age, another is hampered by Saint Vitus' Dance, / uncertain in his balance and his gait, / all three men, crippled civilians . . . " (8). And the poet, the "I" and "eye " enters in the fourth stanza: " I have walked on these artificial, rolled-up leaves, / long-lasting and long out-living the fall of foot and instep . . . " (10). Leaves and the leavings, the detritus of poverty and the sex trade, provide ground cover. The poem keeps returning to the murder with dismay, but it introduces other deaths as well. The poet addresses the victim: "you are not the only one to feel the anger that poverty breeds / you are not the only martyred with nails and kicks" (45); what follows this comment are three stanzas about an African immigrant in Italy beaten to death at the steps of a cathedral in Vincenza, whose blackness then enters the poem, amplifying that other blackness of the third soldier.

Not only the whiteness of the victim marks a difference from Clarke's prose work, the geography invoked does as well. In contrast to the narrow horizons of the fiction, *Sun* moves between Afghanistan, to which the reservists are headed, to Italy and the murder of an African migrant, to his own memories of Cuba, and Barbados, a map that extends the stage of human brutality, although one of the soldiers, the poet notes, "did not reach grade five in school . . . no geography in his head" (26). Arguably the initial declaration that what follows is an act of war itself is geographic, introducing the ways in which states impose themselves on places beyond their borders, and the murder simply an instance of the power accorded the reservists by their uniform.

Most profoundly saddening, even incomprehensible, to the poet is that one of the soldiers is black. In stanza after stanza the poet berates him. He sees his act as a betrayal of his legacy of the cruelty that is slavery and its aftermath, of his mother, a "survivor of the crossing" and of the poet himself, whose skin he shares. "What is the fact of your dignity?" he cries (54).[4]

In her review of *Where the Sun Shines Best,* Maggie Quirt writes: "Shaken by the death of a homeless man in civic space, Clarke's sorrow is boundless, as wide as the country that he holds to account for such violence. In his grief, he offers up a lament that is at once prolonged and restrained" (387). One answer to the question of what poetry allows Clarke that fiction does not is precisely the expression of deep emotion, and particularly the emotion of sorrow, or grief. There are many reasons his fiction cannot accommodate it; these relate especially to the nature of how he draws his characters (who often suffer hopelessness, depression, frustration, hurt, and anger, but whose masculinity would be compromised by sorrow—the one male expression of grief in all his fiction is that of BJ's Italian friend Marco; women weep over the loss of a child or a love, but their emotions do not, of course, undermine them as emotion might a man). Through a setting to which Clarke's fiction occasionally alludes, but in which it is never situated, *Where the Sun Shines Best* depicts a sympathetic continuity between a world of abjection and the poet's witnessing gaze. The poverty of this world is not black; in fact, the park's black inhabitants are daytime users, mothers and children, families. Also, through the poet's address to the black soldier, the terrifying ways in which victim also becomes perpetuator enter the poem; suffering itself does not produce knowledge or goodness. Ironically, for Clarke, the murder victim is a man of words: "he was an editor, a man of words, silenced now, / unable to write his own obituary" (43), or "give the correct punctuation to his narrative" (44). Ultimately, for the poet, however, it is the narrative of the black soldier that finally preoccupies him. The poem closes on him:

> AND YOU are left alone, fumbling with the cord knotted
> round truth and stupidity and loyalty, thick as the dust

> you will breathe in Kandahar, if you get there still, to carry
> out the killing ordered by war, and patriotism;
> witnesses are absent, and there's no "bloody Book of Law,"
> a page of calculus, perhaps, to complicate the ways
> you see things and camels, and humans,
> picked out in our sights.

Clarke's second long poem, *In Your Crib,* comprises a deeply moving reflection on the poet's regrets, also expressing an emotional connection not found in his prose. In tone and structure, an intimate conversation with a son, the poem again is a lament, this time a confession of failure. "There are no Elders," the poem repeats the phrase, "only old men." The refrain, also the title of an earlier short-story collection, comes from Derek Walcott's "The Saddhu of Couva." In Walcott's poem, context, the impact of migration, has robbed the sadhu of his authority and relevance. In *In Your Crib*, however, the poet takes the failure to himself. Listing for his addressee the pantheon of black American leaders of the Sixties whom he knew, he writes: "I was in the company then of 'true-true' Elders. / And I kept silent. Then. And when Stokely said, 'hell, no! / We won't go!' . . . meaning his refusal to obey the Draft; and his refusal to fight and kill Vietnamese, I kept silent . . . " (12). He wonders whether his silence has produced the generational divide, detailed most strikingly in terms of policing, arrests and incarcerations into which the law-abiding poet might have intervened but did not; also in terms of language, a black American slang distasteful to the poet's implied proper and respectful speech; and in music, a discordant rap against the poet's blues and reggae, as well as in no beliefs discernable to the poet.

In Your Crib seems a palimpsest of private and public griefs. The intimacy of address is striking, particularly early on in the poem; for example, the opening: "Do you remember when you climbed / into the shining machine, tugged the shift / to a forward gear, and went in the wrong direction, / into the freshly painted garage? . . . " (1) " . . . I ask you. What you gonna do? / What you gonna do . . . / words finding no object / or predicate. / Again! What you gonna do?" (2) The two are immediately estranged. "I turn my head aside / and my eyes of disregard / filled with disgust, I do not want to see, / to know, to understand. / I do not see your plight, / I do not want to hear your anger" (2). And then again toward the end: "I am a man, old of age and disappointment / for the years that passed me by, and wanting company. / I invited you in, and tried to live with you, / real and lasting; but you have been outliving me, / testing the horror-scope of my life, / and the lens I saw you through" (42). And later: "I cannot carry with me the words and the songs, / and the dreams / I threw away. / My neglect is so cruel, unforgivable / as in ancient times, when 'old pirates, yes, / they rob I' . . . yes, you and I" (48). (*sic*).

Yet the poem's conclusion is both stirring and somewhat ironic. Clarke's 1968 essay "The Confessed Bewilderment of Martin Luther King and the Idea of Non Violence as a Political Tactic" is, as the title suggests, deeply critical of King. In *In Your Crib*, the poet's judgement remains unwavering: "'I have a dream!' / this voice was used to soften / the pain of prison, and not to raise rebellion. / Words were hardly spoken then / before the guns exploded . . . " (15). And nevertheless the poem concludes with a not dissimilarly expressed hope: " . . . and you shall walk / on the same threading buds and flowers / bursting through the rectangular cement squares / you hop from, like in the game of scotch, / exclaiming in a new joy and wonder, / that you are no, living amongst neighbours / who see only the colour of your heart" (53).

Indeed, Clarke's poetic voice has an emotional directness and clarity that his fiction does not accommodate. Or perhaps, poetry frees up that voice, provides him access to it.

In many ways, Austin Clarke's two long poems indeed break from, dislodge, interrogate and transcend the strictures of the script in which his characters live. In terms of Brand's speculations, stripped of the requirement for narrative, the poet can bring into meaningful juxtaposition images, ideas, histories that otherwise may not easily connect. The fabric, or perhaps the melody, that connects, and modulates them, I suggest, is that of sorrow, sorrow songs. If one reads these two long poems with a familiarity with Clarke's work, they seem both reiterative and a gathering of things left unsaid, and they provide a counter melody, a commentary on his work's lower reaches.

RIENZI CRUSZ

Balancing in Silence: On Rienzi Crusz's Engagement with Myth

Aparna Halpé

I have a bad habit. I like to take publicity blurbs on dust jackets seriously. After all, they are distilled critical words of wisdom that should, ideally, make us race to the checkout-counter with a brand-spanking-new book. I must confess that I haven't raced to the counter with Rienzi Crusz's new collection of poems, *Enough to Be Mortal Now* (2009); it has arrived, as it were, through fortunate fate. But I am arrested by the words on the book's dust jacket, in particular by Michael Thorpe's assertion that Crusz "belongs to that older postcolonial generation, including such writers as Walcott and Soyinka, prepared to appropriate the colonial legacy of Shakespeare and English" (1994, 130). The quote comes from Thorpe's early review of Crusz's *The Rain Doesn't Know Me Any More* (1992), a piece that oscillates between a curious critical polarity in which the author simultaneously vaunts Crusz as the "best living Sri Lankan poet in English," and subtly destablizes this assertion by suggesting that his poetry is, in some way, outdated. I find myself fascinated with Thorpe's notion that poetry is, somehow, a thing of generations; intrigued by the critical premise that his approach implies.

It is in this vein that I begin by tracing some of the critical preoccupations with Crusz's work, because to do so is to outline the frequent anxiety that his work produces in critics who would be more comfortable with an aesthetic and matter that was, for want of a better word, resolutely postcolonial. Why does Crusz belong to the "older postcolonial generation"? Because he is comfortable with the so-called colonial legacy of Shakespeare and English? Last I checked, the boys in Wesley College's stunning adaptation of *The Merchant of Venice* (2010) were pretty comfortable with it too, their "appropriation" of Shakespeare a thing of this century, rife with our very own revisions of the paradox of otherness. Yes, perhaps we might say that our colonial education survives intact, well into the twenty-first century. But if it has, it has done so on our terms, submitted to the trials of our histories, and multiplied within the cadence of our many nation-languages.

When Thorpe goes on to suggest that Crusz's "appropriation" of language avoids the "anguished breast-beating" that somehow characterizes later postcolonial writing, he seems to suggest a somewhat monolithic reading of self-reflexive linguistic problematics in Anglophone poetry. This mode of analysis would suppose a fundamental ideological divide (based on generational impulse) between the discourse on colonialism in, for example, Lakdasa Wikkramasinha's "Don't Talk to Me About Mattisse" (1996), and Krisantha Sri Bhaggiyadatta's "The English Wars" (2010). And yet, any critic of Lankan poetry understands that the concerns of both poems are essentially not that different. Thorpe's analysis also suggests that the so-called younger generation of postcolonial poets eschew a certain kind of literary and linguistic tradition. By this token, my own debt to Donne, Eliot, or Rilke would be anachronistic, my poetry bound by conventions that are dismissed as colonial. These observations are only seemingly rhetorical. Thorpe's bizarre evaluation of Crusz's work outlines a fundamental critical anxiety over the function of tradition and inheritance. This anxiety describes a closed circuit in which poetics and politics are determined by a referential engagement with the givens of postcolonial experience. At root, these concerns articulate a more pervasive critical problem—the assumption that writing within a mythopoeic frame invokes an aestheticized cultural metanarrative that fails the political contingencies of a more "radical" nation-language.

Thorpe recognizes that Crusz is a poet fascinated by myth because it affords him a syncretic symbolic frame which extends and interrogates the experience of exile. But Thorpe also seems to assume that the sound and metaphor of Crusz's use of myth does no more than articulate the "undogmatic religion of life." One cannot help but hear the slight condescension that punctuates Thorpe's evaluation of Crusz's writing. Implicit in this evaluation is the notion that Crusz's particular phrase and form is somehow referentially colonial, his theme a rehearsal of exilic nostalgia. If we were to follow Thorpe's hyperbolic ironies, we would relegate Crusz to the annals of postcolonial literature as a poet whose work can be read within the "set pieces" of early postcolonial discourse. To follow Thorpe is to agree that Crusz's poetry has no force of articulation in contemporary thought or soundspace, he is simply the "old" within the new. This is, of course, a rather unfortunate response to a writer whose nonprogrammatic idiom has consistently reworked the substance of lyric voice, whose response to an ever-evolving struggle with the frames of identity politics has been to find form in the vagrancies of myth.

Thorpe is not alone in his strangely polarized response to Crusz. If we return to the early critical evaluations of Cruz's work by South Asian Canadian critics like Arun Mukherjee, we find this polarism extended in various thematic and contextual dualities such as warm/cold, bucolic/post-industrial, and, most specifically, Sri Lankan/Canadian. In *Oppositional Aesthetics* (1994) Mukherjee lauds Crusz for writing the South Asian immigrant experience in lyric gestures that speak to her own critical desire for "meaning," but chastizes him when he forsakes this greater cause to stray into mere poesy. Writing of "Poem in Peacock Blue," she dismisses Crusz's subtly ironic capitulations on colour as images that are "cloyingly rich in their imagery and euphony and short on meaning" (104). Mukherjee hastens to add that at his best "Crusz blends his Sri Lankan and Canadian experiences to make profound comments on both societies" (104) but her assertions of profundity are based on a poem's conformity with her projected frames of reference in relation to both places. Crusz succeeds (where a poet like Michael Ondaatje fails) because he satisfies the rubric of reference that Mukherjee requires of her artist. This predetermined critical bias enables her to make the most remarkable assertions about the referential in Crusz's work. When she asserts that Crusz "subtly criticizes the packaged, programmed life in a postindustrial society and implies that life in Sri Lanka, however hard in terms of material comforts, was more authentic" (105), Mukherjee seems unaware of her own desire to rework

Crusz's nostalgia as authenticity, and she misses, entirely, the complexity of Crusz's own difficult contentment with the package and program of Canadian experience.

Both Thorpe and Mukherjee share an anxiety over Crusz's depictions of Sri Lanka. But, unable to dismiss Crusz's Lankan poetics, they struggle to find a critical language that evaluates his phrase and figure. Interestingly enough, both critics also displace their anxiety onto a pseudocritical evocation of the mythical, suggesting that Crusz's symbolism requires no more than a superficial understanding of myth in order to reveal its true form. Thus, Thorpe casually describes Crusz's theriomorphic symbol of the raven as a "native myth," invoking some vague idea of a Lankan myth that somehow incorporates a tricksterish, dietic raven: "Crusz returns chiefly to reanimate memory, of childhood, as in the controlled nostalgic emotion of 'waif,' or to tap native myth and legend, as in 'he who talks to the raven,' the bird that in his previous volume symbolizes the life force, yet with the darker overtone the poet, now confronting encroaching age, holds in sharp duality." Thorpe does not think to question the figure of the raven as "native myth," and, as a result, misses the weight of Crusz's chosen allusion.

Mukherjee appears to grasp the fact that Crusz draws on a sense of mythopoetics similar to Yeats: "His [Crusz's] poetry is an assertion of his difference. Like Yeats, he has created his own mythology and rhetoric because the available conventions of Anglo-Canadian poetry do not serve his needs. It is this act of self creation that makes his poetry so interesting" (133). However, while Mukherjee readily understands Crusz's mythopoetic impulse, she nonetheless fails to recognize it in the symbolism of the raven in poems from *Elephant and Ice* (1980), remarking merely that " . . . he [Crusz] calls himself a 'crow' . . . a black bird whose frequent recurrence in Crusz reminds one of several West Indian poets" (134). The blind assumption of syncretism, drawn tangentially from West Indian symbolism, is unfortunate, and misses the very point of her earlier assertions about Crusz's generative mythologies.

We might say that Mukehrjee falls into the trap of reading Crusz's symbolism within an easy poetics drawn from her own assumptions on the discourse of identity and racial narrative. Apart from her early acknowledgement of a self-mythologizing impulse in Crusz's work, there is no sustained interrogation of the form, nuance, or ideological persuasion of Crusz's mythical lyricism.

If we take Thorpe's reading of the raven as "native myth" and Mukherjee's likewise problematic reading of the bird as reminiscent of a West Indian "black bird," and use them as frames of reference in a poem from *Still Close to the Raven* (1989), we might start to unravel one of the many misreadings of Crusz's tricksterish mythicism:

> I'm being watched.
> Blue eyes suddenly a torment,
> a torrent of waterfall,
> beauty with a knife between its teeth.
> So once again,
> I must close my black eyes,
> feel my legs
> climbing
> towards the sun.
> Each crag, jutting root,
> now a rung of mercy.
>
> I must move, move
> away from this darkness unasked for,
> or make that second discovery
> of fire: love
> for the tall man with thrusting blue eyes
> seeing nothing
> but a blur of shadowed skin
> a spot on his morning sun. (13)

To be sure, the situation of the poem is simple enough. The casual encounter of racism in the less-than-curious stare of a fellow customer at a coffee shop. However, in the second stanza, the poet suddenly shifts the narrative of darkness, and its invocation of a politics of identity and displacement, into the realm of the mythical. We can only understand that "second discovery" if we understand Crusz's allusive mythography of the raven. And, contrary to what Thorpe might think, this is no myth "native" to Sri Lanka. Neither, I suspect, is it native (except perhaps in the fact that one may find crows in the West Indies as in Sri Lanka) to a particularly West Indian mythography.

Crusz's dark speaker discovers in "fire" the same element of an ambiguous love and violent (if emancipatory) escape that characterizes the Haida myth of the raven who steals the sun. However, Crusz integrally reverses the key mythemes to provoke a revision of the tricksterish raven, proving him powerless against the superior force of the "tall man with the thrusting blue eyes" who sees nothing but a "spot on his morning sun." Crusz's raven has not brought light to the universe, he is trapped in light, no more than a spot in the histories of displacement that make up the story of Canada. His symbol gains its strength from its syncretism, from its identification with the displacement of the First Nations people and the loss of their stories—the myths that have lost their meaning in the tremendous erasure of supremacist histories. To reduce Crusz's raven to a Lankan or West Indian "crow," would be to misread the complexity of the symbol and its palimpsestic frame of reference.

I offer this example of the inherent difficulty involved in reading Crusz's mythopoetics, because it alerts us to the complex symbolic orders that he invokes. While almost all Crusz's critics speak of his lasting engagement with myth, few develop an adequate critical vocabulary that catches the complexity of his narration of myth, and none dare question the function or purpose of myth in his work. If we return to Mukherjee's suggestion that Crusz invents his own mythology (like Yeats) because "the available conventions of Anglo-Canadian poetry do not serve his needs" (133), we encounter a very interesting, if conventional, reading of myth as a structuring principle in the lyric. Perhaps Mukherjee arrives at this reading of myth through a myth critic like Northrop Frye, who defines myth as "the structuring principle in narrative" (1971, ix). In this understanding of myth, we assume that myth is a narrative frame that the poet invokes to achieve a certain emotional or affective cadence within a poem. Mukherjee's observation also draws our attention to the way these cadences, or mythical frames of meaning, are part of literary tradition and narrative inheritance—these are the stories that we swallow, much like the Haida raven swallowed the sun in order to give light to the world. And like the sun, once these stories are released from the artist's grasp and thrown into the world, they gather their own momentum and meaning. They invite new stories, they become seductive and treasonous.

To suggest that Crusz needs myth because he has lost his narrative bearings in his long journey through exile, is to identify the archetypal function of literature to provide a hermetic (not hermeneutical) frame of reference for the chaos of narrative production. It is also to locate the fracture of exile in the many shadows of his narrative inheritance. Perhaps Mukherjee is right, perhaps Crusz invents myth because the conventions of Anglo-Canadian poetry cannot frame a his/story of exile, but I would suggest that this maladaptation to a new poetics and politics of identity allows Crusz to remain more eclectic in his choice of mythic frames, to don renewing masks, and to trace ever more sinuous lines of imaginative belonging from the *Dhammapada* to the twisted Homerics of Derek Walcott. And it is perhaps in Walcott that we gather a closer approximation of what Crusz attempts in his own fragmentary tapestry of myth. When Walcott claims that you "create what you need spiritually, a god for each need" (Burnett 2000, 93), he articulates the capacity of myth to generate new strategies of survival. These are narrative strategies that grow particular to the context in which the poet much refashion his or her craft.

Unlike critics like Thorpe or Mukherjee, Chelva Kanaganayakam has produced a consistent, nuanced critical reading of the poetry that demonstrates, for the first time, the complexity of reading syncretic traditions analytically in Crusz's writing. Significantly, it is Kanaganayakam who draws our attention to a quote by Robert Crusz that describes the poet as "having a cultural identity which is an ongoing process of becoming, never finally arriving" (1997, 10). This sense of "becoming" forms a thematic rhythm through the many volumes and, I would argue, provokes the mythopoeic impulse in Rienzi Crusz's work. In his introduction to *Insurgent Rain* (1997), Kanaganayakam traces a pattern of formal evolution that punctuates Crusz's volumes of poetry from 1975 onwards. Beginning with *Flesh and Thorn* (1975) and *Elephant and Ice* (1980), Kanaganayakam demonstrates the raw power of the early volumes and outlines the concern with loss and private sorrow, and the introduction of the Sri Lanka/Canada polarity in narratives of exile (xx). He goes on to trace tropes of resistance as they appear in *Singing Against the Wind* (1985) and the subsequent volumes, and concludes with the fruition of the difficult processes of adaptation to a new place and politics in *Beatitudes* (1995). Although uncomfortable with the teleological frame invoked in this kind of approach, Kanaganayakam demonstrates the presence of a thematic continuum in Crusz's work, and argues for a critical evaluation that recognizes the subtle shifts and echoes of form that each new volume affords. But, Kanaganayakam also warns against assuming a linear programmatic reading that schematizes Crusz's creative output, suggesting rather a cyclical critical approach that reads centrifugally as well as centripetally:

As Kanaganayakam suggests, tracking the changing thematic spectacle of Crusz's work does not necessarily build an encounter with resonance, but when we allow ourselves the luxury of repetition and recapitulation, we begin to hear the cadence of his symbolism. I would venture to add that such a synchronic frame of thematic reference speaks directly to the mythic element in Crusz's work. It is the Janus-faced aspect that returns to the moment of conception even as it gazes forward to the final abyss.

Enough to Be Mortal Now (2009) is a passionate conversation with a source. Unlike the previous volumes, Crusz's focus returns time and again to the presence of the Godhead in his torturous, all-consuming Muse. Thus, while we encounter the familiar tropes of raven and elephant, and the themes of identity and exile, the questioning voice of the poet turns ever inward to the growing silence of the numinous within himself. And it is this metaphysical struggle, this grappling with season and choice, that makes this collection of poems perhaps the most concerned with the function of the mythic within the poet's individuated symbolic order. A poem like "By the Edge of the Mahaveli at High Noon" (4) obliquely introduces the central issue, the big question, the existential "Why?" that punctuates the silence of most poems in this collection. At first glance, the poem may seem no more than a Lankan pastoral, a piece that captures what Mukherjee calls "the beautiful evocations of Sri Lanka" (Mukherjee 134). But if we read with an awareness of Crusz's particular mythic order, we recognize the function of theriomorphism within the landscape, and the translation of nature in her manifest aspect, into the divine:

> nothing breaks
> the sentinel mood of the great river,
> how sun-fish and minnow,
> crow and heron,
> high noon's lancing glare
> the river's adamant quest
> fashioning this uncompromising story
> with a happy ending:
> the mighty river tumbling at last
> into the ample arms of the Indian Sea.
>
> So why and I here   alone
> by the edge of this great river?
>
> Searching for God
> in this patch of green Eden?
> Answers in the baptism of waters,
> silences to match
> and empty cathedral?
> Realities of life and death
> in the heron's beak,
> faith, like the river,
> at journey's end? (4-5)

Even if the cadence of life is captured in a heron's beak, the poet refuses the comfort of the proffered happy ending. As Adam, alone in Eden, still seeking God, the poet outlines a postlapsarian exile, not just of the paradisical Lanka to which he always returns, but the spiritual exile of the soul now faced with dissolution. If the two great existential questions of this poem are one and the same, they remain untouched by "faith," their syncretic answer, a glimpse of pure form, an archetype before the frames of myth can give us the comfort of meaning.

And the poems in this collection return to silent answers. The volume's title is a tentative answer, a "vesper of an insurgent angel" (97) offered more to the poet's questioning soul than to the silent spiritual "Lord" of the volume's concluding poem (99). Elegiac, in keeping with the tone of his earlier work, this collection bears the insistence of an older Donne brought face to face with mortality. And like Donne, a poet who would claim the last commandment as "love" (Donne 2005, 110), Crusz remains passionately gnostic to the last. The sensuous gambol of old familiars like "Elegy for an Orange" (95) resound differently beside the "fading eyes" of "Wanted" (94) and the anguished death dance of the fading sun man (97). As "Sunless Sequences" indicates, the anguished cadence of Crusz's "mortal" phrase must settle into phatic silence, resounding hollow against the tortuously transcendental permanence of the celestial body:

> Today I write of quagmires,
> deep fissures, of dreams
> that spill blood thick as oil,
> Vespers from the mouth of insurgent angels.
> You stagger with an exaggerated face,
> a knee bone soft as pulp.
> What whirls the blood to epilepsy,
> so darkens the skyline
> as if to frame another crucifixion?
>
> My God, the rose has waited in vain;
> the butterfly is changing its ballerina mode
> to a clumsy tumble of death.
> It is the fourth day
> and you hug your doll of flame
> like a selfish child
> to your ribcage, beyond
> our asking eyes, cold skins,
> your cumulus curtain drawn tight,
> as if for another siesta. (97)

The poet's dream begins in the context of insurgency all too familiar to the Lankan psyche. The image of blood and recalcitrant angels invoke a personal and public hell, their dreams of emancipation from nation and state echoing Satan's protest: "Here at least, we shall be free" (Milton 1821, 242-271). But Crusz draws this public history inwards to his own private tortures—a knee bone softened to pulp, blood staining the sky of a second crucifixion. Of course, we hear Milton and Yeats, even as images of decapitated students and suicide bombers congregate in the failing body of the poet. With such history, God *is* no more than a "selfish child," his sun's nourishing warmth withdrawn for yet another postlapsarian age.

Interviewed in Roshni Rustomji-Kerns's collection of South Asian poets, Crusz calls out, passionately for the freedom to speak the myth of his life: "I plead, I dream of a happy synthesis of cultures, a fashioning of a new mythology" (Kerns 43). And I must ask again, why must a poet plead for the articulation of personal myth? Crusz seems to understand that the mythopoetic content of his work will be constantly subject to a critical process that reduces the multiplicity of the mythic image to the purely referential. And perhaps, it is this dream of a new mythology that makes for such uneasy attempts at sober, if nuanced, critical explorations of the mythic elements in Crusz's work. It is this area of blindness that leaves an otherwise sympathetic and able critic like Mukherjee to lapse into unfortunate universals that would tar all black birds with the same brush. Contentious as it might seem, I would assert that our postcolonial anxiety with mythopoetics has paralyzed our critical acumen to such an extent that we have no vocabulary to negotiate the sound and phrase of Crusz's "new mythology." But if we return, momentarily, to Robert Crusz's early observations on the renewing processes in the poet's journey, we might suggest that such a process of "becoming," of shaping phrase and cadence to sound a new order, requires a poetics that spins out of destruction "a song for those yet to come." (Lincoln 1999, 21) The mythic element that punctuates Rienzi Crusz's eternal traversal of boundary appears, in *Enough to Be Mortal Now*, to unsettle our assumptions about the poet's symbolic orders. The raven and the elephant give way to the white butterfly, the classical symbol of the questing soul and the likewise tragic ephemeral creature who circumnavigates our island to die on its highest peak. The eternal journey of the sun man negotiating each crag of shadow as a "rung of mercy" in *Still Close to the Raven* (13) pauses beside the banks of the sentinel Mahaveli, but if his song shifts to silence, in "Poem for the Faltering Man," in *Enough to Be Mortal Now,* it finds that space once more, in becoming:

> I'm balancing
> on the brink
>
> death and panorama
> around and below.

But faltering legs
dangerous landscape

or final decisions
will not make the poem.

Only supreme electricity
of doubt,

those screaming moments
when wind, muscle and mind

argue
whether to keep me here

alive.

(2009, 26).

This is an updated version of the article "Balancing in Silence," which appeared in Nethra Review *12:01, 2 June 2011.* noolaham.net/project/127/12635/12635.pdf

ANITA RAU BADAMI

Postcolonial Mothering in Anita Rau Badami's *Tamarind Mem*

Asma Sayed

> The cathexis between mother and daughter—essential, distorted, misused—is the great unwritten story.
>
> Adrienne Rich, *Of Woman Born*

Anita Rau Badami's novel *Tamarind Mem* is narrated from two different perspectives: the first half of the novel is told by Kamini, a young Indian woman working on her doctorate in Canada, and the second half by Saroja, her mother in India. Most of the events in the novel are recounted from memory as both the characters remember their past and tell the same story from their own viewpoints. The mother-daughter relationship is central to the narrative. In fact, the story outlines multiple mother-daughter relations, allowing readers to witness not only the intergenerational developments within a family, but also the relationships that are formed as a result of such social interactions. Being a woman and mother raising two daughters in postcolonial India, Saroja negotiates various power relations, the social and cultural impacts of colonialism, and attitudes toward mothering that are rooted both in India's patriarchal culture as well as its colonial legacy. On the other hand, Kamini, who has internalized patriarchal ideals of motherhood and the associated role of women in this society, expects her mother to fulfill socially ascribed roles. Motherhood as an institution is affected by patriarchal powers and cultural oppressions; as such, motherhood becomes complicated for Saroja. This essay will analyze the novel as a maternal text and look at the ways in which motherhood, both as an individual performance and as an institution, is forced on Saroja. The complex intergenerational relationships between mothers and daughters in the novel develop during and after the British Raj. I argue that Saroja's understanding of women's liberation and empowerment is informed by Western notions of emancipation. Thus, as much as she strives to raise her daughters as strong, independent women, her daughters, her husband, and her society do not understand her. Kamini partially recognizes her mother's desires only after she leaves India, and both mother and daughter seem to value each other only when they step outside of the Indian space—either geographically or culturally. Thus postcolonial India is rendered as a space not suitable for women's liberation.

Textual representations of mother-daughter relationships in novels such as *Tamarind Mem* allow readers to understand patriarchal social constructions, in this case those of Indian society, as such relationships function within the framework of broader socioeconomic structures. Such a study is especially relevant in the postcolonial context. As many anticolonial critics have argued (see, for instance, Anne McClintock), women in postcolonial societies have not necessarily become decolonized, since they remain chained within shackles of patriarchy and tradition. Thus, the maternal in postcolonial societies has to be viewed against the background of local patriarchal as well as colonial power structures.

Many postcolonial female authors have focused on motherhood as a theme in their writing. Ama Ata Aidoo, Buchi Emecheta, Julia Alvarez, Toni Morrison, Kamala Markandaya, and Manju Kapur are exemplary of this group. These writers and many feminist scholars (for instance, Adrienne Rich, Andrea O'Reilly, Sara Ruddick), have argued that the institution of motherhood functions within specific sociocultural perimeters, and either rewards or punishes women based on how they perform their roles as mothers. Katrak, in his article on motherhood in fiction, contends that "romanticised images of motherhood commonly propagated by postcolonial male writers, and by the culture generally are demystified in the realistic, often harsh images of mothering by postcolonial women writers" (276). Badami joins this group of postcolonial women writers with her novel *Tamarind Mem.*

Badami is an Indo-Canadian writer of four novels: *Tamarind Mem* (1997), *The Hero's Walk* (2001), *Do You Hear the Nightbird Call?* (2006) and *Tell It to the Trees* (2011). She has contributed to the Canadian literary scene extensively through her continued literary engagement with issues affecting Canadians of South Asian origin. She has been especially known lately for her focus on the *Komagata Maru* and Air India bombing tragedies in *Can You Hear the Nightbird Call?* Her second novel *The Hero's Walk* was a finalist in the 2016 CBC Canada Reads competition.

Tamarind Mem, with its focus on mother-daughter relationships, is a welcome addition to motherhood literature, as stories written by authors of Indian origin focusing on this relationship are very few and far between. Radhika Mohanram, in an article analyzing two Indian stories, laments that "not even a skeletal blueprint exists for the narrative of mother-daughter relationships within the master discourse of Indian fiction. This is not to say that there are no significant female characters in Indian mythology—rather, this particular relationship is just not valorized" (1996, 21). South Asian culture, much like many other cultures, glamorizes motherhood, but values sons more than daughters, thus controlling mothering through patriarchal ideologies. The maternal role is considered central to the identity of women in South Asia. As Jasjit K Sangha and Tahira Gonsalves argue:

> In South Asian culture, motherhood has historically held significant meaning and women's reproductive abilities have been celebrated, through rituals performed in ancient India, writings in religious texts in Buddhism, Hinduism, Islam and Sikhism, and traditional practices of matriarchy in some communities. However, along with this reverence came terms and conditions, steeped in patriarchy, that defined how women should mother. Most notably, that women should aspire to motherhood within a heterosexual marriage, and as mothers, they should be sacrificial and devoted to their families. (2013, 2)

A similar traditional environment is imposed on mother characters in *Tamarind Mem*. Saroja, and her mother, Amma, have been prepared to perform within such socially prescribed maternal roles.

The Mother

The first half of the novel privileges the daughter's account and situates daughterhood at the forefront. However, the second half of the novel presents "a matrifocal narrative," and the voice of the mother emerges triumphant at the end. A matrifocal narrative is "one in which a mother plays a role of cultural and social significance, and in which motherhood is thematically elaborated and valued, and structurally central to the plot" (Podneiks and O'Reilly 3). Saroja plays a significant role in her daughters' lives, and the novel, by the end, clearly leaves the reader with more understanding of her experiences of mothering. However, the reader's understanding of Saroja and Kamini's relationship keeps shifting as much of the story is related from memory. The shifts between mother-narrator and daughter-narrator also signals shifts in points of view.

Saroja's mothering is conditioned by what she witnessed, and struggled with, as a young girl. As mentioned earlier, motherhood is an institution rooted in patriarchy, and thus male-controlled norms and values are enforced on mothering women. Saroja had seen the struggles of her mother, Amma, her grandmother, Putti Ajji, and her aunt, Chinna—all women without much agency. She had desired a different kind of life for herself; she wanted to be educated and become a doctor. However, Amma had insisted that Saroja get married because she did not see any value in education. As Amma explained to Saroja, "A woman can read and study all she pleases, her words mean nothing after all. So why you are wasting your youth and our money? Get married . . . A woman without a husband is like sand without the river. No man to protect you and every evil wind will blow over your body. Listen to your mother" (158). When growing up, Saroja was constantly reminded by her mother that "a woman's happiness lies in marriage" (159). She wonders now if her mother had been happy in her own marriage, or if she would have wanted a different kind of life, but she also recognizes that her mother was no fighter:

> My mother refused to fight for anything. But who am I to say that her life with Appa was unhappy? She framed her conditions for contentment and found them within marriage. My

> father gave her security, a home, the freedom to do what she pleased inside that home. His affection for her was as solid as a pillar and my mother's life grew rich and bountiful twining about that pillar. (216)

Saroja sees that her Amma had no freedom in her marriage as she was totally dependent on her husband. Similarly, her grandmother Putti Ajji was aware that her husband had an extramarital affair, but the only power she had in the situation was to charge a rupee per meal to her husband, who did not eat at his mistress's house because she was from a lower caste. Likewise, Saroja's aunt Chinna, widowed as a child, was not allowed any pleasures of life; as a Hindu woman, she was expected to live a simple life after becoming a widow. None of these women are "outlaw mothers" to use Adrienne Rich's term. And yet, Putti Ajji is criticized by society and her own daughter for even speaking about her husband's affair. As a mother, Putti Ajji ought to have silenced herself; her daughter remarks: "And have you ever thought how we, their children, felt? Those pitying looks from all our relatives. . . . the fault was entirely Putti's" (215).

These women then extended their lack of agency to the next generation because of their fears for their children's well-being. For instance, Saroja was denied any control on her own life whether the decisions pertained to her education or marriage. She was forced into an arranged marriage, and her education was cut short. Her parents were unwilling to spend money on her education. In fact, her education was not valued in a society in which only women's domestic abilities were considered useful. When she came home with her high school diploma, Saroja's father "barely glance[d] at the parchment with its curly black lettering; only [her] brothers' diplomas [were] worthy of his attention" (165). Yet, when her father decided to let Saroja go to college to get a BSc, it was her mother who stood against it. Amma was worried that educating Saroja would work against her, rendering her unfit for marriage. As she said, "A woman is her husband's shadow" (214).

Saroja being the oldest daughter of the household, her sister's marriage then depended on her being married; as per the Indian tradition, a younger daughter cannot be married unless the older one is.

Thus, to rush her wedding, Saroja's family found her a groom fifteen years older than her. Saroja wonders, "Why did my parents have to get me married to this old man? I could have finished my studies, found a job and supported myself. Of course Appa objects to the women in his family working. It demeans him somehow" (187). Saroja's father, Appa, insisted that "only harlots earn for a living" (188). Saroja's wish to be self-reliant was crushed at the altar of tradition and misogyny. She hoped that her life after marriage would provide her with some autonomy.

After marriage, Saroja realized that she had simply moved from one oppressive situation to another. When she woke up the morning after her wedding night, all she remembered was her husband's desire: "I remember the soundless love-making of the night and wonder that my body neither thrills nor cringes at the memory. Perhaps this is because all that I can recall of the experience is my fear and my husband's merciless quiet, his hands moving over me without any tenderness" (199). Saroja's husband had little interest in her except for her body, which served only as a vessel for fulfilling his desires:

> He says I look like a slut when I wear the long emerald earrings my grandmother gave me for a wedding gift—green for a full womb, she said. He sleeps with me on Wednesday night at 21:40 sharp and Sunday same time if his train is in town. My feet tangle in his pyjama for he doesn't like undressing completely. How can I explain . . . the yawning monotony of my life with this man? How do I translate the dislike that rages through me when his voice touches my ears, or his hands brush mine? (212-13)

Saroja resented being married to this "man who ha[d] no feelings to spare for a wife" (216), and her first pregnancy became a burden for her: "It fills the hollow spaces of my body, this child conceived in silence, it squeezes against my lungs, makes me breathless, sends sour belches searing up my throat" (203). Thus, her first experience of conceiving a child brings painful memories to her later in life; instead of savouring the birth of her daughter, Saroja has been left grappling with those moments that do not separate her motherhood from wifehood. She continues to negotiate between her performances as a wife and a mother. And yet, she wants to make sure that her daughters' future is different from her own past. Saroja values her children; in spite of her family's desire for a male child, she at no point devalues her daughters. As opposed to her mother, who "only wanted to see [her] daughters married" (160), Saroja expects to see her daughters educated and working. In a way, Saroja wants to live her desires through her daughters, especially the first-born, Kamini. For instance, Saroja says, "At least one child of mine should get a chance to achieve all that I wanted. It is your duty to keep your mother's head high" (121). Saroja is trying to create a better world for her children. As she does so, she unknowingly prepares them to model Western notions of empowerment.

Saroja believes that her daughters will have a better chance of finding their place in society if they go to English-medium convent schools run by English nuns and learn to speak English like English people. Saroja's valorization of the British is presented at the very outset of the novel. As Kamini says:

> She called all white people angrezi. For her there were only two countries in the world, no matter what anyone else said. This side of the seven seas it was India and across it was Angrez-land, home of the Queen-Who-Never-Shat. Ma had told me, a little sheepishly, that when she was little, she had believed that the Queen of England was so royal that human failings such as the desire to visit the toilet did not bother her. Even as an adult, her devotion to all things British never wavered. Ma regularly subscribed to Women At Home magazine, which cost fifteen rupees per issue. (20)

Saroja uses designs from English magazines to make "pretty dresses" for her daughters (20), and cuts Kamini's hair "to match one of the models" in one such magazine (20). She also makes her daughters read out loud the children's section, "making sure [Kamini] remembered to round [her] mouth over the "w"s and bite [her] lip on the "v"s like British radio news-readers on the BBC" (20). Clearly, Saroja is raising her daughters to dress and talk like English women. When Kamini "refuses to wear skirts above her knees, or sleeveless frocks"—considered hallmarks of Western culture—Saroja thinks that Kamini is "becoming a sanctimonious little nuisance" (240). She wants Kamini to be educated in a convent school, but is unhappy when the daughter becomes like a "nun" reading issues of

Soldiers of God and refusing to wear fashionable clothes.

While Saroja accords her daughters freedom, which she did not have, and aims to educate them so that they may have their own career paths to independence, she also sees those ideals of freedom as possible only within a Western context. Recognizing that English is the language for upward mobility in postcolonial India, Saroja fears that without English education her daughters "will be like the servants' children" (37), and looks for convent schools wherever the family moves. As Kamini explains, "Ma insisted on sending Roopa and me to convent schools, which were always booked full. It didn't matter where we were transferred or how far away the school was, Ma stood in the admission queues and got us in. In Lucknow we went to St Agnes' School, in Calcutta it was Mount Carmel, and in Guwahati it was La Martinière's" (36). Saroja encourages her daughters to succeed; as Kamini remembers "her stories had several messages—study hard, reach for the best, don't be brazen" (126). Despite the fact that Saroja has cultivated feminist ideals, most of her understanding of women's social roles seems to come from reading Western magazines.

In many ways, Saroja is held captive by patriarchal values inherited from her own family. Saroja expects her daughters to get married at the right age. Both her daughters disappoint her: Roopa marries too soon, and Kamini chooses to go to Canada to pursue her doctorate instead of getting married. Saroja regrets, "I have been a modern-times mother and these girls have taken advantage of me" (151). Her daughters have not performed to her expectations. At the same time, the daughters, unable to see their mother's struggles and her isolation, value their calm father more than they do their mother because she is "the witch, the daayin" (226) who disciplines them all the time. Saroja's husband, who works for the Railways is away three weeks in a month leaving her to do all the parenting on her own. She says, "I buy [my daughters] bloomers, petticoats, school notebooks, water-bottles, toothbrushes. Dadda comes home like a magician bearing strange gifts, tales of wonderful things and places" (226). The matrophobic daughter values the economic power of her father till she learns to see her mother as a woman.

The Daughter

Daughters' experiences of "being mothered and [their] perception of motherhood in general, and of [their] own mother in particular, are shaped by the larger patriarchal narrative of motherhood and daughterhood" (O'Reilly 1998, 90). As such, although Saroja has tried to give to her daughters the freedoms that she did not have, Kamini, as a young child, upheld patriarchal ideals about motherhood, which she has internalized through her social interactions. She expects Saroja to perform motherhood as other mothers in her society do. She does not like her mother's insistence on education, or her mother's constrained relationship with her father; rather, she expects maternal behaviour from Saroja. As she complains, "All the way through baby-school, high-school and pre-university, my mother pushed and scolded, her words stinging, buzzing about my head like a crazed bee" (119-20). From the outset of the novel, the relationship between Saroja and Kamini is presented as confrontational. The novel begins with Kamini, who has moved to Calgary, phoning her mother in India; before she calls, she dreads what her mother will say about her desire to go to back to India. When they talk, the two argue about their memories of their past. Kamini thinks that her mother is an argumentative woman who wants to win every debate. As Elizabeth Brown-Guillory says, studies "suggest that when a mother looks at her daughter, she sees herself. She is constantly reminded of her mistakes, yearnings, dreams, successes, and failures. When the daughter looks at her mother, she often sees herself and rejects the image in the mirror" (1996, 2). Kamini's memories of her mother are shrouded—she remembers Saroja as a sharp-tongued woman who was constantly angry with her husband. As a child, Kamini saw her mother as a monster, a "two-headed pushmi-pullyu from Dr Dolittle's zoo or the Ramleela drama woman with a good mask on her face and a bad mask on the back of her head, changing her from Seetha to Soorpanakhi in a single turn" (Badami, 48-49). She reached out to her father, Dadda, to "rescue [her] from the grasping tentacles of Ma's will" (122). Although her father travelled most of the time, and Saroja was left to take care of her daughters alone, Kamini had more respect for her father, whom she saw as "a grownup person who travelled in trains," while her mother simply "yelled and screamed" (11). Kamini failed to understand the frustrations of her mother, and looked at her father as a victim who suffered Saroja's sharp tongue. The work of her father, which was outside of the domestic sphere, was valued more by Kamini. Saroja's constant insistence that her daughters study, get a good education, and become economically independent was seen by her daughter as an impediment to her social growth.

Kamini's view of her mother as a monster is typical of a daughter's matrophobic desire to be unlike her mother. Analyzing mother-daughter relationship, and looking at daughters' matrophobia, O'Reilly writes:

> The daughter must distance and differentiate herself from the mother if she is to assume an autonomous identity as an adult. The mother, in turn, is perceived and understood only in terms of her maternal role, viewed either as devouring shrew or devoted madonna, bitch or victim, her own subjectivity as woman is eclipsed by her maternal identity. The mother represents for the daughter, according to the received narrative, the epitome of patriarchal oppression that she seeks to transcend as she comes to womanhood, and yet the daughter's failings, as interpreted by herself and the culture at large, are said to be the fault of the mother. This is the patriarchal narrative of the mother-daughter relationship. (O'Reilly 1998, 70)

Kamini feared becoming like her powerless mother. Furthermore, Kamini, influenced by the society that she inhabited, was judgmental about her mother's actions. As a child, she kept an eye on her mother's actions and reported them to her father. Kamini knew that her father disapproved of Saroja going out on her own; he reminded her often about her domestic duties: "Your place is in this house, not out there in the streets doing social work and gossip while my daughters run around like gypsy beggars" (Badami, 84). The reason for Kamini complaining to her father had much to do with Kamini's constant desire to be with her mother, because she did not like to be left with Linda Ayah, the housemaid (85). Clearly, as a child and a teenager, Kamini was unable see her mother's need for freedom.

Nor did Kamini like her mother's insistence on adopting English ways. When she was made to read stories about Nora and Tilly, Kamini "wished that they had different names—Gauri and Geetha, perhaps, or Mini and Bani." Kamini thus wished her stories were Indian. She got her Indian stories from her father, Vishwa, who read to her stories from the *Ramayana* and the *Mahabharata*. Irrespective of her interest in Indian stories, Kamini decided to go to Canada for further education. It is only from this distance that Kamini's matrophobia recedes, and she is able to see how motherhood was imposed on her mother: "Ma, [was] guilty at not having fulfilled the role that had been scripted for her, annoyed at being coerced into playing it" (147). She now realizes that perhaps her father "was to blame for the person Ma had become. He shut her into rooms from which there was not even a chink of an escape" (147). However, this realization occurs only after Kamini has left India, that is, only in a space outside of the traditional India is the maternal appreciated. When she looks back at the events of her childhood, she realizes that as much as she and her sister, Roopa, resented their mother, perhaps the mother was not to be blamed:

> Ten years, ago, I had felt a simmering resentment against my mother. I believed that she had wronged Dadda with her rigid anger, her unkind words. I refused to acknowledge the years that Ma had spent being a good wife, looking after her daughters, supervising the household, making sure that Dadda got his meals exactly as scheduled. How bored she must have been. . . . Perhaps Dadda was to blame for the person Ma had become. He shut her into rooms from which there was not even a chink of an escape. He himself had left again and again, and every time he came back, he needed to be readmitted into lives altered daily during his absence. (147-48)

The relationship between Kamini and Saroja reaches some level of understanding only after it is outside of the geographical space that they both inhabited. On the other hand, after the death of her husband, and once both her daughters have left, Saroja decides to travel around India via train. Ironically, as she travels from one town to another, Saroja is tracking the footsteps of her husband as well the legacy of the British. The Railways are a reminder of India's colonial era. Her train journey in a "women only" compartment allows her to open up to other women, who listen to and empathize with her. Within the sphere of the Indian patriarchal space, Saroja could only be a "tamarind mem"—a woman with a bitter tongue and a temper that was not acceptable to her family. But, on the train, she is a "storyteller, a weaver of myths" (266).

Anita Rau Badami's *Tamarind Mem* depicts many sides of the mother-daughter relationship, and serves as a critique of patriarchal structures in India. The mother and the daughter, Saroja and Kamini, fail to understand each other when they are within Indian cultural and physical space. Kamini appreciates her mother after she leaves the geographical boundaries of India, and her mother is able to speak freely only within the confines of a British-built Railway systems. The mother-daughter relationship fails to foster in postcolonial India; the bond develops at a distance and through the intervention of Western feminist ideals.

H NIGEL THOMAS

Trauma and Melancholia in H Nigel Thomas's *Behind the Face of Winter* and *No Safeguards*

Dannabang Kuwabong

> Our lives here, what have they been? What exactly have they been? . . . Somewhere, I heard that the magic in promised lands ends once they've been reached, that promised lands should never be reached. . . . While in St Vincent, Ma saw Canada as a promised land; and, in Grama's eyes, Canada was promised land for Paul and me.
>
> H NIGEL THOMAS, *No Safeguards*

The utopian Canada imagined by Africaribbean people that Jay surmises in the above epigraph is, however, a dystopia for Africaribbean immigrants. Not so long ago people of African descent were considered undesirables in Canada because they were seen as belonging to the "myriad ethnic communities [that] are not particularly favoured by the larger white community over others" (Hintzen 2001, 10). The speaker in Claire Harris's *Drawing Down a Daughter* (1992) makes this clear when she states that though the Caribbean islands have colour and class biases, "it's one of the few places in the world where black children can grow up socially and politically secure" (69). She asserts, "[I]magine anybody in Trinidad of any race or culture telling you that your child didn't pass those British exams the islands use because she was culturally disadvantaged?" (69). Contrarily, in Canada "every cliché [then] is underlined, . . . in the assumption of moral superiority, in church, and more important, school, it's the funny look in the eyes of your best friend's mother. . . . It's in the playground teasing, in your first date. . . . It's overwhelming you come to accept it yourself! . . . At least till you get militant" (70). Systemic racism in Canada generates melancholic and neurotic behaviours, especially among Africaribbean Canadian youth. In *No Safeguards* (2015) and *Behind the Face of Winter* (2001), H Nigel Thomas crafts narrative representations of how Africaribbean Canadian children respond to these issues.

In his review of *When the Bottom Falls Out and other Stories* (2014), Horace I Goddard describes Thomas as one of "the luminaries of Canadian literature" whose biomythographies propel "us through . . . psychological as well as geographical journey[s] through the persona[e]'s childhood development[s]. . . . [through] time, space, and place, [and] mythologizing . . . growth from childhood to manhood" (Goddard 2002). Psycho-spatial journeys, what I call shifting identities, are the cultural adjustments Africaribbean Canadian children must make in Canada, while also dealing "with [issues of] parent/child relationships, racism, [and] police brutality." In addition, Goddard argues, Thomas agonizes over "the exploitation of immigrant women [mostly the mothers of these children], family survival in a hostile environment, and the role of the church in providing hope in a place where harshness only seems to abound." Relatedly, Veena Gokhale interprets Thomas's work as interrogations of traumas initiated and enforced by "the complex impact of colonization and its aftermath, both tangible and less tangible, on [Afro] Caribbeans . . . on those who . . . emigrate, showing how race, class, gender and sexuality come into play, within the context, to further disempower and trap people" in these immigrant locations (Gokhale 2015). My reading of *No Safeguards* and *Behind the Face of Winter*, hence, focuses on Thomas's explorations of these traumas and melancholies among Africaribbean Canadian teenagers struggling to establish their individual and group identities in Montreal.

I contextualize my reading of these novels within the conceptual frame that has been defined by Linda Hutcheon and Marion Richmond, echoing WEB Du Bois's theory of "double consciousness" (Du Bois 1994, 2): "Doubleness . . . the essence of [immigrant Canadian] experience. Caught between two worlds, the immigrant negotiates a new social space; caught between two cultures and often languages, the writer negotiates a new literary space" (9). Du Bois argues that "double consciousness" (2) is caused by a "sense of always looking [at themselves] through the eyes of others, of measuring [their] soul[s] by the tape of a world that looks on [them] in amused contempt and pity" (2). Hence, doubleness among Africaribbean Canadian youth, depicted in Thomas's Canadian novels, generates trauma, melancholia, and personality disorders. Éric Paquin asserts, Thomas presents "nouveaux arrivants en quête d'une existence millieure, confrontés aux embûches de l'intégratíon, á la nostlgie et á l'enfermement du ghetto, voire á des religions réparatrices mais impiyoyables . . . ils sont noir, anglophnoes et transplantés dans une sociéété blanche francophone" (2015, 147). Correspondingly, Hugh Hodges claims that *Behind the Face of Winter* unveils the traumatic and "the destructive secrets we keep, even from ourselves, and the spiritual cost of keeping those secrets. It is also, of course, a story about the harshness of the immigrant life Pedro faces in Montreal—bad housing, bad jobs, unaccommodating educational systems, racist police forces," leading toward the greater struggle "for self-respect and self-knowledge in an often brutally hostile world" (Hodges 2001, 20).

Undoubtedly, therefore, the multiple traumas, alienations, and melancholia among Africaribbean Canadian youth are further complicated as these youths languish in aspirational shrinkages and produce "tasteless sycophancy, or [drive them] into silent hatred of the pale world about them and mocking distrust of everything white; or wasted itself into bitter cry" (Du Bois, 2). To Thomas, "alienation from . . . community, and, to some extent, from their authentic selves," (Gokhale 2015) intercepts full participation in the Eurocentric Canadian space. Cecil Foster expands the debate of the alien culturescape to include ecological alienation as a cause of trauma and melancholia among Africaribbean Canadians: He writes, ". . . [Canada] can be heavenly when it wants to be, a place to raise my kids. . . . But alas, . . . one pleasant evening does not mean an end to a harsh winter. The unusual warmth can be just a delusion . . . a something to lull us into dropping our guard" (1996, 2). Such environmental unpredictability engenders desolation among Africaribbeans [as they struggle] "to maintain a shred of [their] corporeal standing so that something verging on exchange may occur" (Bartkowski 1995, xxiii) in Canada's nebulous multiculturalism. Melancholia, then, as argued by Min Zhou (2001, 202-203), is enhanced by hidden exclusionary barriers within the racialized hierarchies of multiculturalism. Subsequently, to many Africana Canadians, the political rhetoric often is not complemented by policy implementations, exacerbating an already toxic atmosphere of cultural alienation, bitterness, and melancholia (Kasinitz et al 2001, 268-69). Undeniably, Canada's multiculturalism policy yields multiple benefits to Africaribbean Canadian communities. It ensures that both federal and provincial governments support the promotion of Caribbean cultures, thus promoting inter-cultural tolerance. Nonetheless, Foster highlights the issue of the unpredictability of European Canadian moods, and argues that this engenders confusing identity cartographies among so-called (in)visible minorities, which then "both confer[s] and limit[s] . . . identity, shape, and place" (Bartkowski, xxv) within these communities. Thus, Thomas's writing represents Africaribbean Canadian "community, family, and kinship relations that make for [them] a web, a network" (xxv). Proportionately, therefore, Thomas repositions his characters to help them develop their "encounter(s) [with Canadian] authority and learn [their] own relation to it, to own it, too, if only for [themselves]" (Bartkowski, xxv) and their communities. Exploring that sickness among Africaribbean Canadian youth is Thomas's critical engagement with and response to their brokenness. Like Jay in *No Safeguards*, Thomas uses "writing to explore [the Africaribbean Canadian] sickness" (222) of melancholia through negotiated identities.

In *Behind the Face of Winter* and *No Safeguards* Thomas explores the negative consequences of alienation and melancholia, nostalgia, and the futility of restorative recuperation of disappeared Africaribbean identities. In *No Safeguards* Jay laments, "*it is expensive to preserve what's already dead; and those who do so do so alone; and in the end they too give in, from wisdom or from weariness*" (294). Expanding on his argument, Jay writes: "*Of course we mourn all deaths, . . . And mourn we must, for death of whatever sort discords, dishevels, dismembers* (294) [Emphasis in original]. Caren Kaplan postulates that immigrants suffering from alienation also suffer from "unresolved anger toward . . . [their original identities that have] been irrevocably removed" (1996, 33). Unable ". . . to resolve the conflict [of separation] or express this anger openly without guilt; . . . [they] remain[s] in a state of acute loss. When this particular kind of latent aggression is turned inward, against the self, melancholia sets in and becomes a preoccupying state that replaces or fills the space left by . . . separation" (33-34).

Unquestionably to some degree, Paul and Pedro suffer from this malaise as they struggle through their identities' confusions in Montreal, battling against racist essentialist stereotypes that delegitimize their corporeal presence in Canada. Moreover, confronted with no available context of reception—cultural, economic, political (Stepick et al, 233-235) with provisional "situation[s] . . . of received interpretations . . . " to develop personal and group identities (Simone de Bouvoire 45, quoted in Kasinitz, 287), they wallow in abjection at the margins of society. Circumstantially, therefore, Thomas interrogates these harsh realities confronting Africaribbean Canadian youth, and suggests temporal reliefs through paradigms of shifting identificatory practices (Walcott 1997, xiii) such as religion, gangster life, education, and travel. These identificatory practices include, first, asserting specificities of cultural, ethnic, national and linguistic differentiations among Afro-Caribbean immigrants; and second, rejecting the tendency to lump all Black groups into one no matter whether they originate from the Caribbean, the United States, or Africa (Foster, 15-30). Significantly, both Walcott and Foster agree that the lack of differentiation among different African Canadian groups, renders them into an absent presence, a visible invisibility (Walcott, xiii).

Pedro's melancholia and neurosis in *Behind the Face of Winter* and Paul's psychosis in *No Safeguards* are evidence of their multiple alienations generated in the contradictory contexts of reception (Portes and Rumbaut 1996; Stepick et al, 2001). Stepick et al contend that the "context of reception and parental capital [are] contributing causes to [Africaribbean] youth identity crisis" (232-233) in America. Thus, though Pedro is Isabellan and Paul and Jay are Vincentians, their lived experiences in Canada must be read in the context of their reception in Montreal. First, Pedro experiences a negative reception in his encounter, on the flight from Isabella to Montreal, with a white Canadian woman. Thinking Pedro is Haitian just by being black, she declares that Haitians "didn't understand Canada and had many problems" (73). This is revealing. She adds, "For one thing, nobody understands their French" (74). Yet when Pedro bold-facedly asks her whether she speaks Haitian Creole, she grins sheepishly, avoids the question, and commends Pedro on his excellent English. Pedro recognizes the lady's role as a cultural gendarme using language to keep "blacks as undesirables" and out of Canada.

The encounter initializes a feeling of cultural dissonance in Pedro. It suggests that assimilation must first surmount cultural dissonance with its concomitant parent-child conflict and potential for diminishing academic achievements (Harris, 123, Stepick et al, 254-258, Kasinitz et al, 287-294). Cultural dissonances and negative contexts of reception and alienation in the two novels unleash in Pedro and Paul repressed anger and melancholia, which transmute into verbal aggression. Alienated from their Canadian and Africaribbean societies, they periodically erupt into unsettling confrontations with their equally frustrated immigrant mothers living in poverty in Canada. Secretly they may even share the shames and disappointments of their mothers. Isis's and Anna's low human capital as unskilled and undocumented immigrant workers creates the ideal stage for the series of problems that affect them, personally and in their relationships with their sons (Foster 1996, McCleod 1995, Pearlman 1995, Portes and Rumbaut 1993, Schultz 1993, Wharton 1986). In addition, both Pedro and Paul openly resent their forced separations from hitherto healthy filiations with their Caribbean-based grandmothers. Systemic racism undermines any positive results that migrating to Canada may have offered these children. Africaribbean Canadian parents, "located in the ethnicized construction of difference" (Hintzen, 10) in Montreal, endeavor to teach their kids one set of cultural values, while the education and legal systems teach them different values that torpedo the parents' Africaribbean norms (Foster, 103-112): Caribbean music forms, food, hard work, religion, respect for elders, and the expanded family. Certain nuanced racist interpretations of these boundary markers are negatively stereotyped as "reference schemata in the cognitive construction of [Africaribbean] people as . . . cavalier, fun loving, heat, sex, bacchanalian, accommodating" and not to be taken serious (Hintzen 17).

In *Behind the Face of Winter* and *No Safeguards*, Pedro, Paul, and Jay initially contend not with Canadian racism but with their social demotions, predicated upon their mothers' low socio-economic statuses in Canada compared to their almost middle-class locations back in the Caribbean. Shocked and disillusioned, Pedro feels an ambivalence and anger toward his mother and Canada, exacerbated by the mother's filthy one-room basement "apartment [which] stank. Its last occupant must have been incontinent. The air-freshener [his] Ma had sprayed in it mixed with the other odours to create a nauseous, sweetish vegetable rot . . . . I sat on the sofa and raised a cloud of dust that set me sneezing" (76). Ma's feelings of shame at her conditions makes her unreceptive to Pedro's concerns. Similarly, Jay says in *No Safeguards* that "Paul's ambivalence for Canada and, indirectly, his hatred for Anna [his mother is] because she had brought him here" (103). Paul's spite toward his mother is clear: "'Fathom that,' he told her on the anniversary of our arrival. 'Just fathom that!'—sounding like Grama—'We left our comfortable home for this'" (103). Disgusted with the apartment in Montreal, Paul is nostalgic for what he left behind in St Vincent. He romanticizes and mourns the loss of his comfortable dwelling: "From our back porch we used to look out over the sea, watch the sunset, the fishing boats, the fishermen pulling their seines, the plovers diving in and out of the water" (103). He quips, "You and I used to go through Grama's orchard raiding the fruit trees and spend long hours in the sea all year around. Now we live penned up like prisoners, our clothes reeking of our neighbours' cooking—in a country that's frozen for half the year. Open your eyes Ma! This is no place for us" (104). He makes an impassioned appeal for the lost life-giving, and emotionally nourishing natural and social ecologies of St Vincent, and rejects his new Canadian home as a sociocultural and ecological dead end, a hoax. He asks: "Why are we here. Ma? Can you tell me why we are here? So you can earn a living emptying bedpans? It's a dying, if you ask me" (104). Paul's problem here, then, starts with cultural dissonance enhanced by his conclusion, as cited in Walcott above, that "the [white] people we live among, they're just as cold, colder than the climate" (104). Paul's statement echoes what Foster calls the "emotional cost of immigration" (103), an emotional trauma leading to death and not to life (104).

Decisively, cultural and ecological dissonances inhibit any positive concept of reception in these boys. Their actions confirm that cultural dissonance "includes children not conforming to parental guidance and potential role reversal between parents and children claim better knowledge about the host culture and society. Accordingly, cultural; dissonance frequently results and intensifies parent-child conflict" (Stepick et al, 233). Thus, the fact that such "social psychological outcomes that include youths' ethnic identity, self-labelling, perceptions of discrimination, lower self-esteem, and [. . .] depression" represent the more salient areas of cultural dissonance between them and their mothers (Stepick et al, 233-34, Kasinitz et al, 286). Their "diminished second generation educational achievement," (Stepick et al, 234) especially in the case of Paul, testify to the consequences of cultural disarticulation and estrangement, not just racism (234). Foreseeing this, Sister Agnes in *Behind the Face of Winter* counsels Pedro on how to conform to certain norms of Africaribbean Canadian behaviour in order to succeed. Unable to respond to their sons' emotional and cultural needs on their own, both mothers get the help of other Africaribbean women, though the sons do not openly accept this help. Sister Agnes instructs Pedro, "You mas' lissen to yo' mother, you know. When the young people-them come here, them think them know how the lie'o the land stay, some o'them even think is them own it, and 'fore you can say bullcow, is jail them reach, and when them get them trouble is we parents what have for do all the running around . . . " (78).

Analogously, when Paul in *No Safeguards* throws his vitriol against his mother, Anna, in front of her visitors, Madam J and her daughter Anita, Madam J takes him on. "So you're the woman that's filling Ma's head with foolishness," Paul said. "Boy, how you so out-o'-place and bull-buck so? Me is a grown woman. Me is not your age-mate. If me didn't know Sister Kirton, me wouldo' think you didn't get no broughtupcy" (145). Madam J tells Paul, "You mekking fun o' me or what? You better praise God you not under my roof." . . . "I would o' blister your backside morning, noon, and night" (145). The statement reveals parental frustration at their inability to discipline their children in Canada in the Caribbean way. Though Paul fails to respond to Madam J's assertiveness he still gets away with his cruel mockery of Anna, knowing very well his mother cannot give him any corporal discipline: "Boy you is

Lucifer ownself? What wrong with you? Why you giving Sister Kirton so much botheration? Why you make evil hollowing you out like woodlice inna dead wood?" (146). He is exposed as an insecure boy, a: "force-ripe man . . . [who is implored to] stop 'busing poor Sister Kirton" (147). Paul masks his vulnerability with hackneyed phrases such as: "I think we can be friends as long as I protect my neck. You're kind o' cooler than I thought. . . . Know something: I *love* to go head to head with you. It's fun" (147). He wishes his mother could be cool like Madam J or Grama. "Ma, all you do is work, work, work, . . . Ma, you need a life. Do like Grama. She's cool: she gets together with friends, and they have a good time on a Saturday night. Every bank holiday she'd take us off somewhere and we'd all enjoy ourselves" (96). Madam J, who reminds Paul of his Grama, earns Paul's respect.

In contrast to Anna, Isis never retreats from investing emotionally and financially in her son Pedro's future. She draws on male father figures, Erskine and Solomon, to help guide Pedro through the webs of alienation and melancholia. Both Anna and Isis also appeal to Africaribbean religions as cultural aids to program their sons against the inimical effects of racism and poverty. Thomas, of course, critiques the superficiality of these religions. He judges them as con-games in which the "masses are duped into silence through fear and religious manipulation" (Goddard 2002). Nonetheless, Thomas recognizes how "traumatizing alienation from one's community could be" because as he stresses, "Your community is your psychic mirror" (Gokhale 2015). Thomas agrees with Foster that the Africaribbean Church in Canada is a sanctuary of temporary relief (Foster, 53-62), a place that both Paul and Pedro in their melancholic moods and nostalgia deprecate as predatory. Hence, while spouting atheism, Thomas nonetheless, recognizes the positive roles of Afrocentric spiritualties. He acknowledges that these spiritualties offer refuge for "their members [to restore] the dignity denied them in the broader [Canadian] society" (Gokhale). What Thomas critiques is fundamentalist Methodism and its negative impact on the self-perception of Africaribbean people, more especially its demonization of gay sexuality. In *Behind the Face of Winter*, Pedro, still fresh from the Caribbean, feels culturally smug and superior to his mother and rejects the communal and supportive values of Wayfarism (178) until much later (184-185). To Pedro, they should never have "come to Canada to become [. . .] Wayfarian" (85). Pedro is ashamed of his mother's social retrogression (85), the reality of which she defers through her Wayfarian spirituality. However, unlike Anna in *No Safeguards*, Isis asserts her maternal authority over her son, derived from her role as provider, and reads him a riot act (85) when Pedro disrespects her. This is the type of parental authority that Paul wants Anna to exercise.

Isis's actions stem from the reality that Africaribbean youth in Canada are over-liberated from parental authority, yet over-policed. This creates familial and social dissonances leading to misdirected rebellions against parents and society. Here, parents become immediate and first targets of their anger and resistance against a racist educational system designed to delegitimize and control them. Confirming this, Thomas expresses his shock "at the attitudes of some of my colleagues [in a high school he briefly taught]. [He] could not believe that someone who had gone through university and had a teacher training could be overtly racist. Then I saw it with my own eyes" (Goddard 2015). Thus, in *No Safeguards*, the racist educational system stifles Paul's high academic performance. Back in St Vincent, Paul had schooled with "the children of the island's wealthiest and most accomplished people. In Montreal, his classmates were children of tradespeople . . . factory workers, drug pushers . . . and he was shocked by their sparse knowledge and paltry vocabulary" (98). His unhappiness at his social decline generates an initial dislike for his classmates for "[listening] only to vapid music and gab about stupid TV shows" (98). Worse, the black kids, Paul asserts, "eat, dance, talk nonsense, and harass their teachers. Klunks!" (99), exhibiting negative stereotypic semiotic markers that produce and legitimate their social marginalization (99-100). Returning the honour, they label Paul "geek, nerd, wimp, fag," for trying to achieve (98). Unsurprisingly, therefore, "The joyful, humorous Paul, who never missed an opportunity to best me, was gone. At the end of September, he told [Jay] he hated being Black" (99).

Paul's early self-directed racism originates in "mistakes that wounded Paul, mistakes he had no coherent language for. Anna and Paul didn't know each other, and she didn't know she should have spent those couple of years forging a bond with him" (97). His bitterness is rooted deeply in his desire for the recognition that is impossible in Montreal: "In Montreal, . . . nobody knew he was Ma Kirton's Genius and wouldn't have cared. In St Vincent, his schoolmates and the community lionized him for his brilliance" (97) after he won the spelling bee contest. In Montreal he is just another inconsequential and pathological underachieving black kid. Exacerbating this situation of inconsequentiality, the trauma of being bullied by the "older boys in his class [who] were roughing him up at lunch and recess and constantly threatening to beat him up," especially in the case of Alfred (101-102), makes Paul wet his bed, further shaming and angering him. To mask his shame, Paul becomes what he earlier despises (103). He takes and pushes drugs (124-125), and has to borrow $200 from Jay to pay off gang-related debts (148-149). For initiation into gangster life, and to prove his masculinity in the public arena, he tries to steal from a jeweler, vandalizes bus shelters, paints graffiti on walls, ends up in police cells a few times (124). At this point both Jay and Anna fail to see Paul's struggle with alienation, melancholia and emotional decline toward suicidal psychosis. He confesses to Jay, "If I like continue as I'm going, don't you see one day she'll [Grama] read terrible things in the papers about me, or hear about it on radio or TV? I'll run away if I have to, I can't continue like this, Jay. I can't. You can't imagine the nightmares I'm having. I'm ashamed of myself, Jay. If I don't change, I'll kill myself before they kill me" (149). Paul masks these insecurities through violent masculinity performance, coupled with destructive remorselessness for his mother. In lucid moments, he confesses, "Jay, you are right. Ma never deserved to be treated the way I treated her. . . . I hated myself, and I hated her for having had me. But if I am as heartless as you make me to be, I would prefer to be dead. And there were many times I wanted to be dead, since I was 12. At times I deliberately courted it" (233). To him, "Not writing to Ma or mentioning her when I wrote you was just a continuation of my behavior before I left. You're right. I wanted to make her suffer . . . " (223). He suffers from the melancholia caused by the loss of both material comforts and social status and privilege by coming to Canada, translated into a devalued sense of self (Foster 103-104). For Thomas's protagonists, their "trauma ensues when [they] . . . discover they've exchanged home for something worse" (104). Paul's melancholic belligerence encodes the unspoken pain recorded in his poetry and journal entries. Writing is Paul's way of coping with his emotional chaos (Pennebaker 3-13) traced back first to maternal rejection in his infancy, second, to his relocation to Canada, and third, to his reduction in social standing.

I have indicated above how the Canadian family law complicates and inhibits Africaribbean family relations in Canada and promotes rebelliousness in Africaribbean Canadian children against their parents. Paul exploits this and justifies his cruelty to his mother when he labels her an unfit mother who must yet put up with him until he turns eighteen. Hurt, and recalling abuse by Paul's father prior to Paul's birth back in St Vincent, she retorts: "You got that part right. I should have listened to your grandmother and never had you" (142). Paul, not expecting this, emotionally crumples and cries out: "*The information I needed.* Thanks [. . .] You should have. I HATE MY LIFE AND I HATE YOU" (142). Paul rediscovers his voice and screams venom at his mother: "Finally! The answer I've been looking for. I suspected it the moment I came here. You should have aborted me. My asthma is psychosomatic. Because you rejected me in the womb. Good thing you unloaded me unto Grama. At least I had nine years of decent parenting" (142). Unable to confront his demons and unwilling to understand his mother Paul blames her for all his problems (222). But following Anna's death, and after Jay reprimands Paul on his unwarranted cruelty to their mother, Paul weeps in repentant desperation, realizing he has lost the chance to ask his mother for forgiveness: "Paul swallowed and wiped his eyes on his sleeve. 'Everything sucks. Everything.' He swallowed again, trying to suppress his sobbing. 'Everybody hates me'" (143).

Unlike Anna, Isis strategizes to ensure that Pedro succeeds. Her vigilance saves Pedro from becoming another black male underachievement statistic: "On the steps sat two black teenage boys, they were smoking and tapping their feet and rocking to reggae that came from a boombox placed one step above the step they sat on" (101). He is reminded of Isabellan youths' mimicry of African American youth. These "shiftless Isabellan males strapped themselves to their boomboxes, sported dark glasses, smoked cigarettes with gangster antics and affected a menacing, undulating, catlike style of walking" (101). Of course, Pedro's early dis-identification with these shiftless youths makes no difference to white Canadians. In Montreal, there is no difference between African American youth and Africaribbean youth. Thus, Isis's worries, which foreshadow Pedro's racial alliance with the black group comprising Alfred, Zachary, Hollis, and others (122-24), are justified. Pedro, like Paul, cannot deal with the racism he faces in the classroom and on the playground, and is angry but unable to fight back. He subsequently projects this unresolved rage against his mother, the soft target. But unlike Paul, Pedro has father figures and male role models in Mr Erskine and Solomon, who guide him away from the racially prescribed pathologies cast upon young African American males: "They are cast as fools or criminals" (Harris 126). These roles are monitored to ensure that black kids never aspire to positions reserved for white kids—doctors, lawyers, engineers, professors, etc. "What rewards [black kids] is being 'cool'; the way they dress, the sports, they play, and the cheap entertainment they provide" (126). Based on these observations, academically oriented bright kids like Paul, Jay, and Pedro are frustrated.

Ghettoized and pressured by a racist educational system, Pedro and Paul are pushed to hang out with the Black youth groups, in order to survive in Canada's socially stratified population. For Pedro, in *Behind the Face of Winter* the initial encounter with racism at school is with Mrs Black and Mr Johnson. Though they both recognize Pedro's brilliant academic record, evidenced in the excellent scores in the test designed to fail him, they place him in a lower grade (111-117). Similar to Paul's debilitating experiences with the white and Asian kids in *No Safeguards*, during which his crooked teeth, and his presumed Black male hypersexuality become fair targets for racist taunts (102-103), Pedro's frightening brush with white male kids in the first day in school displays how racism works at every level of Canadian society, and unravels the psychological traumas inflicted on Africaribbean male youth within Canada's violent masculine and rape culture (Buchwald, Fletcher, and Roth 1993):

> I walked around aimlessly. At one point I found myself in the middle of a group of about fifteen white boys. They were eyeing me. A stocky one with freckles, shoulder-length blond hair wearing jeans and a jean jacket more faded than the others, said mockingly. "Monn, is you a Jamaican, monn?" There was something odd about his face. . . . "You got dough?" the stocky

> one asked, his eyes glassy, morning-glory blue. A third one I couldn't see said, "Now what kind o'foolish question is that, Dreyfuss? You ever see a rich nigger yet, unless he's a pusher or got long fingers or something?" (126)

Pedro innocently attempts to sidestep the racist slurs and is accused of being unreceptive. "You know who we are, man? Ask yer nigger brothers who Nations is, man, and watch them shit in their pants. I have a mind to take you in to the john and make you suck me off" (126). According to them Pedro has "got the right size lips" (126) and "big, round ass" (127). The white kids disappear suddenly when a much tougher though smaller group of black kids appear in the horizon and come to his rescue. "I broke out of the circle and followed the black boys until I got to a side entrance, ran up the steps, and reentered the building. I . . . was aware for the first time how frightened I was" (127). Thus, Pedro's first day at school is an introduction to two sets of hostile and opposing social groups.

Acceptance into the black inner group is not gratuitous. It is predicated on the coded performance of urban black youth subcultures (131-32). Mervyn asks Pedro: "Them white boys start fee gee you trouble yet?" (134). Hollis also offers him a hand of friendship and protection: "Well if ever they start, le' we know, oui, ". . . "Last year I crack a chain over one o' them fellas head and now when them fellas see me, is clear they clear the space, oui" (134). He stresses that Pedro's security lies with the black alliance: "If they see you hanging 'round with we, they going leave you alone. But if you is like that Oreo that is president o'the student council, we will le'they whale yo'arse, oui, if you pretend you better than we" (135). Hollis's message of undifferentiated group aspirations and performance is clarified in Alfred's (218-221) words, affirming academic underachievement as a black thing, as a resistance to mental colonization and domination (159-160). Alfred then draws on the Oreo-cookie complex to both shame Pedro and to draw him into compliance with this ideology of defeat (188-189, 213, 219-220). Unhappy initially, Paul nonetheless adopts the group as a stop-gap measure against insanity. He, unlike Pedro, however, does have Erskine and Mr Solomon, who agonize over this destructive blackface mimicry (140-141). Erskine and

Solomon tell Pedro; either to embrace Hollis and his group's ideology of failure and regret it later, or accept their advice and guidance. Hollis and his gang represent an alliance with destructively ill-conceived and undifferentiated notions of black masculinity (131-190): violence (127-28), porn, sex and homophobia (155-168), profanity (162-63), music, dance (131-32), drugs (161), theft (155, 204-206), and prison terms (219). Pedro's mentoring by his Isabellan Grandma, Mr Sam, Mr Erskine, and Brother Solomon enables him to withstand the seductive pull of Hollis's group. Interestingly, Thomas exposes and problematizes cultural jealousies between Africaribbean kids born in Canada and those coming fresh from the Caribbean. Alfred, an immigrant child, appears in both novels and is angry that Canadian-born kids believe they have proprietary rights to define how Africaribbean Canadian kids must behave. These jealousies destroy any illusions of unity among them in Canada and often lead them to truancy, criminality, teen pregnancies, depression, and suicide. Thus, Hollis and his gang, jealous of Pedro's academic achievements, frame him for a store theft. He is arrested, taken to a police station, and brutally sodomized with a baton and forced to perform oral sex (204-213). As a consequence, Pedro develops a better understanding and appreciation of his mother's, Agnes's, Erskine's and Solomon's moral choices. But singed by his negative experiences, he ends up uncertain about his identity and is unsure of what he can do with his master of arts degree. At the end of the novel, early signs of psychosis manifest. Contrastingly, Paul is not so fortunate. Though like Pedro he is also rejected by his father and mother in infancy, and spoilt by a dotting Grandma, he has the disadvantage of having been deluded to think he is upper class in St Vincent, only to be demoted in Montreal to a lower-class status. Lacking positive role models and mentors, Paul tries to fight back not just against racism, but also against his gay sexuality, which Jay and Pedro both share, through the public performances of stereotypical black male youth masculinities.

Buried deep in nostalgic yearnings for the loss of their roots, impacted by the deaths of their grandmothers back in the Caribbean, and crushed by their disillusionment with a racist Canadian system against which they feel powerless, Pedro and Paul become psychotic. However, not to be seen as painting an overwhelmingly gloomy picture of Africaribbean

Canadian youth, Thomas counterbalances Paul's errantry with Pedro's and Jay's academic successes. They are capable of handling their inner homosexual struggles well. The three characters in the two novels are set together to perform a three-sided exploration of the shifting identities that Africaribbean immigrant gay boys must struggle through in a racist and culturally alienating Canada.

Thomas offers no healing praxes or easy escape paths in these texts. He does provide these paradigms of healing in *Spirits in the Dark* and *Return to Arcadia* as I have argued elsewhere. In *Behind the Face of Winter* and *No Safeguards*, Thomas focuses solely on the diasporic conditions that destroy the psychological stabilities of Africaribbean Canadian gay youths. He avoids rehashing the evils of history and focuses more on the consequences of immigration. These novels, as Goddard asserts, centre Thomas squarely in the Canadian literary landscape without erasing his Africaribbean connections. Moreover, by inserting the psychological consequences of Africaribbean Canadian gay sexuality, Thomas forces and expands the debate about Africaribbean silence and hostility toward homosexuality. His work, set both in the Caribbean and in Canada, becomes his act of rebellion against the hypocritical silences of Canadian society against racism in literary circles and against Africaribbean communities' resistance to an open dialogue on male homosexuality. His "desire is to strip away the mask(s) and send probes into the darkness beyond . . . by the imagination" (Gokhale 2015, xii). By probing the darkness that threaten to engulf Africaribbean Canadian youths, Thomas unveils their strengths and weaknesses and projects a roadmap that potentially opens up more frank discussions among the respective communities about their children's struggles. He also is able to demonstrate without exaggerated romanticism that Africaribbean culture is necessary for the mental balance of these youths in a Canadian cultural landscape that often denies its validity.

CYRIL DABYDEEN

Cyril Dabydeen's Amazing Corpus

Frank Birbalsingh

Born in Guyana (formerly British Guiana) in 1945, Cyril Dabydeen was educated in local schools and worked as a school teacher before migrating to Canada in 1970. He gained a BA from Lakehead University, an MA from Queens University, and a Masters in Public Administration, also from Queens. Not only has Dabydeen worked for the federal government and the Federation of Canadian Municipalities, but he has also given hundreds of literary readings, participated in numerous conferences, and produced an astonishing total of thirty books: thirteen collections of poems, nine volumes of stories, four novels, and four anthologies. His total literary output surpasses that of his cousin, David Dabydeen, who settled in Britain; and the Dabydeens are only two among a growing diaspora of Guyanese and Caribbean authors living today in major metropolitan English-speaking countries.

Cyril Dabydeen served as Poet Laureate of Ottawa, from 1984 to 1987, and he received a Lifetime Achievement Award for Excellence from the Guyana Council of Canadians on May 29, 2010. He won the Guyana Prize for Fiction in 2007 with his novel *Drums of My Flesh*, and was nominated for the International IMPAC/Dublin prize in the same year. In some of his early publications, including poem collections such as *Goatsong* (1977), *This Planet Earth* (1979), and *Elephants Make Good Stepladders* (1982), Dabydeen displays an array of postcolonial subjects and diasporic themes that stand guard in his books like sentries warning readers of risk from postcolonial diasporic dangers like displacement, exile, and homelessness.

In the poem “Encounter,” in *Goatsong* (1977), the persona contrasts himself with Rima, the fictitious wood nymph of WH Hudson's novel *Green Mansions* (1904) and sole survivor among her indigenous people in the Amazon forest shared between Venezuela and Guyana. While Rima is happy in familiar, paradisal surroundings, Dabydeen's persona twists and turns in “the snake's belly” since “[n]o one is here / to help me” in a “red world” where all he can hear is: “the / crunch-crunch / coming from your side of paradise” (1). In contrast to Rima's contentment, Dabydeen's persona is harried by feelings of exclusion and abandonment.

“Grosse Isle,” another poem in *Goatsong*, takes on more tragic ramifications of immigration through an event in Canadian history, in 1847, thousands of Irish people, fleeing famine in their own country, died from a typhus epidemic at an immigration depot on Grosse Isle, in the Gulf of the St Lawrence river. Dabydeen writes: “They perished / forty thousand / from across/ the sea - / all immigrants / trying to start / a new life” (17). If this stark statement of horrific, historical fact in “Grosse Isle” seems too matter-of-fact or unfeeling, it identifies hopeful and positive economic motives in the immigrants.

Another poem, “Citizenship,” focuses on the ethnicity, when a Caribbean immigrant in Ottawa confesses: “I have been here [in Canada] seven years / Yet the same question / Where do you come from? / I'm identifiable / I'm differentiated” (33). Instances of racism appear frequently in Dabydeen's work and, even more so, in the writing of his African Caribbean contemporaries Austin Clarke and Dionne Brand.

By 1994, when Dabydeen's tenth volume of poems *Stoning the Wind* appeared, he had lived for more than twenty years in Ottawa and travelled widely, as hinted in many references in his poems, especially to places in Canada, because of his job with the Federation of Canadian Municipalities; but an immigrant's ethnic perspective is seldom absent, often in instinctive recollections or comments about Guyana and the Caribbean, or Third World issues such as South African apartheid, which was hotly debated shortly before Nelson Mandela was freed from prison in 1990.

"Officialdom" in *Stoning the Wind* assumes a tone almost of weariness, rather than anger when the persona reports a reaction from one member of "an audience of bureaucrats" (34) to his reading of one of his poems: "At our table we were amazed at how well / you [Dabydeen] read that poem, considering English / isn't your language" (34). Dabydeen's persona balks at the insult since he grew up in an English-speaking, Caribbean colony, and he imagines himself "holding up a flag like a distress banner / . . . being stateless / or permanently self-exiled" (34). Suppressed anger is mixed with bitterness and a helpless sense of futility betraying the apparent permanence of an alienating, immigrant identity that sticks to him in his new home, Canada.

In 2004, in his introduction to *Imaginary Origins: Selected Poems 1970 - 2002*, a collection from ten of his previous poetry volumes, Dabydeen reflects on the predicament of "my sense of having been born with Guyanese and Caribbean sensibilities—and now living in Canada for most of my adult life" (11). He speaks of internalizing "Caribbean as well as Canadian temperaments and landscapes" and the possibility that he has found his "truest poetic self in the crossing of boundaries, and the necessity of looking in different directions" (11). He also combines "my diasporic and immigrant selves" and is aware of a "sense of being Janus-faced," while he draws "on the feeling of having a heterogeneous or even a hybrid consciousness as an artist" (11).

The notion of hybridity deriving, in this instance, out of colonial history, gets to the heart of Dabydeen's writing. As a descendant of indentured, plantation labourers in Guyana, he is the product of an environment of African slavery, which lasted from the early 1600s to 1838, and Indian indenture, which lasted from 1838 to 1917. Although, by 1945, the year he was born, slavery and indenture had long disappeared, their effects of indigent poverty and poor living conditions lacking basic services or amenities rankled because they still prevailed in the Guyanese countryside, including the author's birthplace, Canje, a sugar plantation in Berbice, which is remembered both for the Dutch sugar plantations that flourished for nearly two centuries before the British took over, and the first major African slave rebellion in Guyana, in 1763.

The rebellion was brutally suppressed, but the injustice of colonial exploitation persisted at least until the poet's childhood. In 1953, the results of national elections, expressing the democratic will of the whole Guyanese population for the first time, was abruptly quashed by the British colonial rulers of Guyana. In recognizing the peculiar quality of Caribbean landscapes and temperaments, and the heterogeneity of hybrid Caribbean consciousnesses, Dabydeen acknowledges features of an environment to which people of darker skin colour were transported, first from Africa under slavery, and then from Asia under indenture, as labour for exploitation by white European overlords. Hybridity is a mechanism to cope with the inveterately mixed nature of Dabydeen's colonial, cultural inheritance, and the primacy of themes such as race, colour, class, ethnicity, and exile.

Dabydeen's hybrid Caribbean consciousness is seen in sixteen poems from his 1997 volume *Discussing Columbus* that are included in *Imaginary Origins* (2004). Speaking in the voice of Columbus, through an oxymoron in the final line of "Discussing Columbus," the poet's phrase "a deserted but peopled land" cleverly exposes the dubious nature of Columbus's achievement in "discovering" a place where people already existed. Dabydeen's implication of discrepancy in the accepted worldview of Columbus as a hero resists a view sanctioned and authorized by European colonizers, and resistance is a feature of hybrid consciousness. Hybridity is not mere versatility in choosing a variety of subjects, but a more instinctive, almost compulsive urge to question by switching regularly from one topic or point of view to another.

Themes of race or colour and ethnicity or exile dominate Dabydeen's stories as they do his poems. Characters generally shift from place to place, either within the Caribbean, or from the Caribbean to Canada, and from Canada to the Caribbean and Guyana. Because of Canada's superior economic resources, immigration is usually one way, from South to North, but there are visits to the South by Canadian officials and businessmen, and by returning Caribbean immigrants. In his third volume of stories *To Monkey Jungle*, the action of the title story unfolds entirely in the Guyanese countryside. The narrator is a young Guyanese employed to kill insects in his district, while the main action is about a sort of psychic duel, half serious and half playful, between the narrator and Dobbs a rather mysterious Canadian who is possibly a scientist dealing with snakes. Dobbs is believed to live in segregated dwellings with other white expatriates on a nearby sugar plantation. To the narrator's female co-workers, Dobbs, as a white foreigner, is something of an enigma who comes from a land "of sheer ice and snow" (21) where "people had unhappy expressions on their faces in winter as if they were expressing pain" (21). To these Guyanese women, Dobbs might as well have come from Mars, so alienating is their picture of him, his country, and Canadians generally.

Since Dobbs is an expert on snakes, it is strange that it is the narrator who comes to blows with the dreaded rainbow snake, a partly mythical creature that takes shape from the branch of a tree. It is stranger still, after the narrator kills the snake, that Dobbs suddenly collapses, fussing and frothing at the sight of the dead snake, although he does recover quickly, and is expected to return home to Canada later. Tensions of hybridity or, at least, differences between Dobbs and the narrator, or between Canadians and Guyanese have abundant potential for insights about race, colour, immigration and exile, which are imparted a whimsical air from the magical realist mode of narration. For instance, thoughts of romance and jealousy that hover tantalisingly between the unnamed narrator and one of the younger, female workers, Minnie, and between Dobbs and Minnie, appear so much more tempting because of their whimsicality. One isn't surprised when they come to nothing in the end.

"Berbice Crossing," title story of Dabydeen's fourth story collection, is named for the Berbice river that also gives its name to one of Guyana's three counties. While the term may refer to a literal crossing of the river by ferry or boat (nowadays by bridge), and Dabydeen's story relates one instance of the narrator taking part in an actual race to swim across the river, the author's systematic alternation, throughout the story, of scenes or discourses referring to Canada on one side, and Guyana on the other, suggests a decided preference for the title "Berbice Crossing" as a metaphorical journey taken by immigrants between two sharply contrasting milieux, Berbice, Guyana or the Caribbean on one hand, and Canada or the US on the other.

One section of "Berbice Crossing" opens with a reference to Magdalenenburg: "Down the full length of the Canje, a tributary of the Berbice: Magdalenenburg, where the first real slave rebellion in the Caribbean took place in 1763. Slaves crying out: Who will liberate us?"

(107). This is followed by a phone call from the narrator in New York to his mother in Guyana: "A telephone pole leaning over, wires dangling close to the (Hindu religious ceremonial) jhandi pole, red flag fluttering for Hanuman. Is it a symbol of revolutionary communism, the British troops wonder? Cheddi Jagan do you hear?" (107-108). Then the narrative switches back to the telephone conversation between the narrator and his mother, before introducing yet another reference to Guyana: "Mud, swamps, rice fields. Ethnic strife with Indians and Africans asserting ownership over this place (108).

When, in a passage of only about one page, the author intersperses crucial items of Guyanese history such as the slave rebellion, and the forcible dismissal of the first fully democratic government of Guyana led by Dr Cheddi Jagan in 1953, within the course of one long-distance telephone conversation, he produces exactly the type of impressionistic or telegraphic narrative that comes out of a hybrid consciousness. While this narrative style pegs the author's fiction firmly down to a realistic history of Guyana, it also enlivens history with the significance of competition between imperial and national ideologies, heightened by the poetic imagery, rhythm, and fluency of the author's prose.

The Wizard Swami (1985, 1988), Dabydeen's first novel, first appeared in India, in 1985, before being republished in England. *The Wizard Swami* is a light-hearted romp, with scenes of hilarious ethnic farce, and characters and episodes reminiscent of VS Naipaul's first novel *Mystic Masseur* (1957). Like Naipaul's Pandit Ganesh, Devan, the young Indian protagonist in Dabydeen's novel, also aspires to distinguish himself within his rustic Hindu community in Guyana, by joining the All-India League, the premier Hindu organization in Guyana during the first half of the twentieth century.

As in Naipaul's novel, in which Pandit Ganesh's humorous saga lays bare individual failings of envy and pride, or social foibles of deception, hypocrisy, and cunning in Trinidadian society, Devan employs deception and cunning in Guyana, even if his machinations turn out to be less successful than those of his Trinidadian counterpart. While Naipaul's success in *Mystic Masseur* spurs him to perfect techniques of humour and satire that greatly inform the portraits of Trinidadian society in his future fiction, the relative failure of Devan as a social climber in *The*

Wizard Swami seems to have the opposite effect on Dabydeen, whose humour remains less caustic than Naipaul's.

There is scope for humour and satire in Dabydeen's second novel *Dark Swirl* (1988), with action that unfolds in a rural Guyanese community steeped in raw superstition and unsophisticated practices, but the social foibles of Dabydeen's characters are regarded as misfortunes foisted on their colonial, Caribbean community by a harsh legacy of slavery and indenture that saddles them with supernatural belief as their most effective mechanism of coping with real problems and circumstances in everyday life.

Dark Swirl centres on a ten-year-old boy, Josh, whose heightened sensibilities equip him with an intuitive ability to communicate with the supernatural: "They [the community in *Dark Swirl*] could hear in the wind echoes of an ancestral past of indigenous men and women [Amerindians] fleeing into the bushes; of sugar-plantation owners, white-white who buried slaves alive under silk-cotton trees with their own dead so their kind would be served even in the underworld; of voodoo brought from Africa to these shores; of jumbies manifesting from smelly hovels; of backoos who worked in the sugarcane fields in the darkness of the night with an efficiency no man could match; of a plantation owner riding on a majestic white horse, dragging a heavy chain behind; of Moongazer straddling the road, head a pillar in the sky, silently watching" (24).

The main preoccupation of the rural Guyanese community in *The Dark Swirl* is with one fearsome mythical creature, the massacouraman, that inhabits their creeks and waterways. Everyone is terrified, except Josh, whose unique gift of intuition gives him access to the monster, until an unnamed white stranger arrives with a similarly mysterious gift. There is little action in the short novel of only ninety-two pages, and lines between fact and fiction, reality and the imagination, are deliberately blurred as in the fiction of Wilson Harris, whose relentless probing into the folklore of the Guyanese Amazon, over many decades, is an obvious influence on Dabydeen.

The life and death of the massacouraman in *The Dark Swirl* are both mysterious. At the end, the creature is simply reported dead by the white stranger, who is himself feared dead, until he suddenly wakes up and, as the narrator suggests, cannot make out whether he has been dreaming: "the leviathan, the thing they called the massaacouraman, which had dominated the creek for so long in the solitary eye of the imagination . . . was palpably flesh as well as spirit" (89). Rather than reflecting Naipaulian humour or satire, *The Dark Swirl* boldly adopts a narrative genre more akin to the sombre, brooding meditation of Wilson Harris on ancient mysteries, generated but still firmly locked in the dense tropical vegetation of the Amazon.

Drums of My Flesh, Dabydeen's longest novel, offers the author's most convincing study of diasporic themes of displacement, alienation, and exile. The novel is nourished by elements from the author's family history, namely, bruising relations between an alcoholic husband and father and an abused wife and mother who relies on her skills as a seamstress and support from her mother to keep body and soul together. It all happens in the county of Berbice during the 1950s and 60s, years that coincide exactly with the author's own early adolescence. Framed in a structure of magic realism, the narrator, like the author, is an Indian Caribbean immigrant living in Ottawa, who relates his life story to his daughter Catriona, whose mother is a white Canadian. The hope is that her father's narrative will smooth over the difficulties produced by her mixed inheritance.

In the novel, Gabe, father of Boyo, a Guyanese immigrant living in Ottawa, is an alcoholic who abuses his wife Dee, causing her to flee periodically with Boyo and his younger brothers Dev and Anand, from their home in Brighton, on the Corentyne coast, to her mother in Canje. Grandma's home provides a refuge, with Dee constantly glued to her sewing machine, earning money for an independent life with her sons. But all is not privation and pain. Boyo and his brothers pay occasional visits to their father in Brighton where they catch crabs, observe farm life, and mingle with their father and his mother whom they call "Ma." The boys also encounter Fatima, their father's mistress, described as his "consort," who "appeared and disappeared at will . . . Something instinctual being renewed or relived each time they were at it" (137). In Brighton, most of all, the boys meet Gabe's cherished friend and counsellor—Jaffe, an old, blind Muslim who believes he is a descendant of Alexander the Great and, in the rich tradition of Guyanese eccentrics, is fondly regarded by Gabe as a prophetic figure, a legendary world traveller and "an eternal witness to all the world's beliefs" (81).

After the narrator's mother remarries, two more children, Stan and Sarah, are born, but trouble erupts not only between Dee and her second husband, but also between Gabe and Fatima, who finally leaves, making it possible for Gabe also to remarry. This portrait of Indian Guyanese peasant lives disfigured by poverty and endemic violence is corroborated in fiction by other Indian Guyanese authors like Lauchmonen (pseudonym for Peter Kempadoo) and Rooplall Monar. Like *Drums*, action in Lauchmonen's first novel *Guiana Boy* (1960) is also enacted on the Corentyne coast, through scenes of similar physical hardship and struggle, despite which, dexterously, Lauchmonen summons notes of bucolic rusticity. Monar's stories, however, even with plots that unfold in the county of Demerara, confirm Dabydeen's version of struggling family relationships and rough-and-ready living on Guyanese sugar plantations until the 1960s.

Not surprisingly, the author whose work compares most closely to Dabydeen's is Indian Trinidadian Harold Sonny Ladoo (1945-1973), who was born in the same year as Dabydeen, immigrated to Canada in 1968, and lived in Toronto. Ladoo's first novel *No Pain Like This Body* (1972) provides perhaps the most faithful fictional representation of Indian Caribbean agricultural workers that we have so far. Nowhere else is the daily elemental struggle for survival by Indian Caribbean labourers depicted with such unflinching authenticity, in such richly inspired, figurative language. Ladoo's scatological denunciation of immigrant experiences in his second novel *Yesterdays* (1974) is also one of the most incisive studies of Indian Caribbean anomie that we have.

Dabydeen's literary productivity is one thing; another is his ability to keep abreast of the work of fellow writers in four anthologies. The most recent of them, *Beyond Sangre Grande: Caribbean Writing Today* (2011), is the most impressive. In terms of race, colour, class, and ethnicity, the Anglophone Caribbean is probably as diverse as any other region in the world, and immigration just as endemic, yet *Beyond Sangre Grande* fully achieves its chief aims to provide a contemporary view of its literature without any: "generational divide" (xii), to select examples "giving the reader some sense of the tradition we have come to know" (xii) and to observe the overriding criterion of "aesthetic quality" (xii). Older writers like Lamming and Naipaul are not missed because Selvon, Walcott, and Brathwaite are there, as well as a welcome number of female Caribbean authors.

It is not entirely fanciful to imagine the influence on his writing of Dabydeen's lifetime residence in Ottawa, Canada's capital city and seat of government, where official Canadian policies are debated and legislated, for example, multiculturalism and the right of immigrant families to enter Canada, both of which were introduced during the 1970s by the Liberal Party led by Pierre Elliot Trudeau. In the story "Bearing Gifts" in Dabydeen's most recent volume *My Multi-Ethnic Friends and Other Stories* (2003), university students, including foreign students, discuss feeling displaced in Canada; but even those who are born in Canada are uncertain about where they really belong: "Helene added that every [Canadian] province was her home, though each seemed like a separate country to her" (82). In the end the concept of home seems mythical: "It was really about where one's forebears came from, if with gods and goddesses only" (80).

CHERAN

In Times of Upheaval: Cheran's Poetic Trajectory

Chelva Kanaganayakam

This essay is the introduction to the poetry collection You Cannot Turn Away *(2011), edited by Chelva Kanaganayakam. Unreferenced poems quoted here are from this volume.*

A recent poem by Cheran, written sometime after the carnage of May 2009, which marked a radical shift in the ethnic politics of Sri Lanka, expresses a deeply subjective and nuanced response to the contemporary scene, using a diction that is shorn of all embellishment, and is both allusive and suggestive despite its self-consciously epigrammatic style:

> Parched ocean
> Silent land
> Nameless kin

This untitled poem, translated here by me, remains a challenge to any translator, largely because for the Tamil reader the original suggests a great deal about the specific cluster of events in Mullivaikkal in the northeastern region of Mullaitivu that culminated in the defeat of the LTTE in May 2099. Although the poem, even in Tamil, remains abstract and generalized, for the reader who knows the cultural and political scene and is competent in the original language, the specificity and intentionality are abundantly clear. The poem expresses a deep concern about cultural loss, occasioned by violence, dispersal, and death. A more literal (although very effective) translation of the poem, which appeared in a recent collection of poems, reads in the following manner:

> the sea is without water
> tamil is without land
> kinship is without a name (Ravikumar 28)

Here the translation is more expressive of a particular moment of violence, upheaval and fragmentation. A sea without the translucence of water is reminiscent of Macbeth's famous line: "multitudinous seas incarnadine, making the green one red." The sea (a recurring trope in Cheran's work) is a site of struggle but also one that suggests comfort, life, and livelihood. In the second line, the translation draws attention to a specific kind of cultural identity where the land and landscape are associated with both language and ethnicity. Mullaitivu is one of the many places where Tamils lived for centuries, and yet the poem asserts that this moment of violence has deeply affected the linguistic and cultural identity of a people as a whole. Given the widespread presence of Tamil-speaking people today in various lands, the line is deliberately enigmatic. In the final line, there is an ominous projection of the future, a time when kith and kin, dispersed in alien lands, will fail to recognize each other, resulting in a community of "familiar strangers." My own version is, admittedly, more generalized and abstract, largely because Cheran's poetry, for the most part, oscillates between the specific and the general. The fact that the poem lends itself so well to both versions is in itself a measure of the richness of the original and the strength of Cheran's poems in general.

For those who are familiar with Cheran's poetry, this poem (and for that matter, almost all of his more recent poems included in the final section of *You Cannot Turn Away*) would appear to be both familiar and surprisingly different. They are familiar in that they continue certain thematic preoccupations that have been quite central to his work from the beginning. Issues of cultural identity, political stability, nation and nationalism, diasporic life, fragility of human relations, and many others run through his entire work. The recent poems are different in that they recognize the need to use a very different diction, speak with a different voice. Gone are the lilting rhythms of his early poetry and the modernist narratives of his later work. May 2009 marked a watershed in political life, and the poet's work seems to imply that the poetic imagination, responding to the present, cannot simply rehearse the forms of the past. Noticeably absent are certain kinds of metaphors that are present in his earlier poetry. Poetic forms that seemed necessary and relevant in the past are no longer effective, and the poet alters his style to give expression to a different sense of the world. Cheran's struggle to understand and relate to the political vicissitudes of his time must be seen together with his self-relexivity and his search for adequate poetic forms.

At the very outset it is important to recognize that Cheran is the product of a conflict-ridden Sri Lanka. This might be stating the obvious, since it is common knowledge that in Sri Lanka from the 1970s until the defeat of the LTTE in 2009, the dominant concern among the people, both Tamils and Sinhalese, was ethnic conflict. Toward the latter part of that decade, unrest among the Tamils, particularly the youth, became increasingly common, eventually leading to the rise of militant groups among the Tamils that sought violent means to counter what they saw as the hegemony of the state. While Cheran himself was not affiliated with any particular movement, and was often critical of the stances adopted by various political organizations, he lived and functioned in a culture that was deeply politicized. Politics was thus the overarching concern of many writers of this time, including Cheran. Unlike poets who started writing earlier and encountered the transformation of society in the 1970s and 1980s, Cheran came into his own as a poet during this time. Politics and violence in the country shaped his craft, his imagination, and his consciousness. Any serious evaluation of Cheran's poetry should take into consideration the effect of having to live and function in a world in which politics and the violence it gave rise to permeated each and every aspect of life. Cheran's poetry demonstrates the process of not only learning from the literary traditions of the past, but also reshaping them to address the urgency of the present. Both the politics and poetics of his work are determined by the turmoil and upheaval of conflict.

It is common knowledge that some measure of political uncertainty was often present in postcolonial Sri Lanka. Even a cursory look would confirm that manifestations of political dissatisfaction were common, both among the Sinhalese and the Tamils. The ethnic conflict of 1958 and the insurgency of 1971 were obvious cases in point. The Tamil poets who wrote in the 1960s and 1970s were not unmindful of the political backdrop and the effects of political decisions on social and cultural life. But political uncertainty was only one aspect of a new postcolonial nation. There were many other concerns for the Tamils that were seen as urgent, including caste, class, economic disparity, and regionalism. The poets of these early decades thus worked with a number of concerns and their poetry was inevitably eclectic and sometimes hermetic as well. Their poetry was socially conscious, and often quite progressive, but it implicitly endorsed the notion of aesthetic distance.

Cheran grew up in this context, and his early influences included the work of his father, Mahakavi, whose poetry was path-breaking in its ability to merge a distinctly modernist sensibility with traditional metrical forms of poetry. Cheran himself acknowledges in an interview the deep impact of his father's poetry, and his own habit of memorizing large chunks of his father's poetry and then reciting them in public places. He also claims that at a certain stage in his career, the influence became less prominent, as his own voice became clear to him (*Kalachchuvadu* 11-32). Among other things, his father's poetry taught him the rhythms of language and the prosodic forms of traditional Tamil poetry. Orality was central to Mahakavi's work, and if Cheran's poetry continues to have a strong oral dimension, it is probably because he recognized the potential in Mahakavi's work to appeal to a large audience. In any account that relates to Cheran's intellectual genealogy, it is necessary to emphasize that it was his father who played a major role in steering a tradition of conventional poetry to one that was socially conscious and one that accommodated the idiom of ordinary speech. Mahakavi's poetry and his plays enabled a distinct break from the tradition of Tamil poetry from Tamil Nadu in that it was neither experimental nor entirely conventional, but one that was receptive to both in a distinctly Sri Lankan way. Mahakavi was writing at a time when poetry was still the possession of a small group of writers and critics, and his own accommodation of the local and the folk was shaped within the framework of conventional poetry. Even in a famous poem such as "Therum Thingalum," where the speech rhythms interact most forcefully with poetic diction, the effect of artifice leans toward convention. To say this does not take away from the major contribution of Mahakavi; it simply highlights the fact that he belonged to a particular time and a particular place.

Cheran also records in other places how his consciousness was shaped by Marxist thinkers, both local and international, whose perspectives were particularly meaningful in a class-conscious and caste-conscious Tamil society. Says Cheran:

> My association with an important representative of the Communist Party and a charismatic speaker Comrade V Ponnambalam gave me a sense of the importance of contesting both class and caste structures. During this period, around 1973-74 two of my poems appeared in the newspaper run by the Communist Party . . . . In 1975-76 Mao's writing became available. Another close friend N Murugadas was actively involved in the Communist Party led by Shanmugathasan. He was a passionate reader of literature as well. Through him I was introduced to both Mao's writings and the literary journal *Kasadathapara.*[1] (1984, 11)

Marxism, however, remained one aspect of his early vision. The lyricism, gentle irony, sense of community and belonging, and the love and eroticism of his early poetry are a testimony to the multiplicity of the early 1970s. This was, however, a time of learning for Cheran, a time of shaping his craft. The lyricism of some of his early poems is a clear indication of the influence of a poetic environment that may have been influenced by ideas of social reform but was equally conscious of the need for aesthetic distance in poetry.

If one were to think of *Maranothul Valvom*, an anthology put together by Cheran et al in 1984 as a turning point, the title itself (We Live Amidst Death) alerts one to a complete transformation of sensibility. This was one year after Cheran had published his first volume of poems, titled *Irandavathu Suriya Uthayam* (The Second Sunrise), which points to the burning of the Jaffna Public Library.[2] The title is significant in that it signals a particular urgency, a direct engagement with the political and cultural context of the time. The introduction to *Maranathul Valvom*, written by Cheran, is a valuable guide to his thought and his poetry. In this he records the impact of living in a context in which the extraordinary had become the ordinary. Among the observations that Cheran (one of the editors who writes the preface) makes, one needs to note in particular that the collection was seen as part of a larger cultural scene in which literature, together with other cultural forms, was being embraced by the public as a constitutive element in a larger framework that involved nationalism and ethnic identity. As he puts it, "in our context, poetry is hardly for silent reading or for the sole enjoyment of intellectuals. It must appeal to the common person" (Cheran 1984, 11). Poetry, together with fiction and drama, now had a much more vital role to play, and this collection points to a radical shift in sensibility and in poetic practice. A new vision, a new style, and a new urgency had entered the literary scene.

The next collection, *Yaman*, published in 1984, sets the tone of despair and death that now becomes a crucial element in life. During the last three decades, Cheran's personal and public life have undergone many changes, and his current status as an academic and a diasporic poet in Canada are a far cry from his early life in Sri Lanka, but he has remained very much a "political" poet, a product of a time of political and cultural upheaval in Sri Lanka. Although Cheran has written about love and exile, for instance, and writers such as Sundara Ramaswamy have alluded to the strength of such poems (2000, 210-214), his ongoing concern has been with the impact of politics in the social and cultural life of the Tamil people.

Cheran's poetry as a whole, however, defies any easy compartmentalization. From the very beginning, the challenges were many. In the first instance, it was never very easy for the poet to define his own role within the conflict-ridden state. While the commitment to some form of Tamil identity appears to have been a common thread in all the poetry, the particular contours of this commitment were far from clear. In the murky waters of ethnic strife, a simple binary along ethnic lines was never easy. The poet demonstrates in several poems the need to see beyond ethnicity to human relations, to friendships, and to the suffering on both sides. Equally important, the resistance among militant groups was never seen as unified. In his own life, Cheran's refusal to stand behind any particular stance meant, quite often, living on the edge. There is a poem in his corpus that is significantly titled, "A Poem That Should Not Have Been Written." It is a poem that expresses the deep disillusionment of a militant group attacking Sinhalese civilians and the awareness that even the most lofty ideals might mask cruelty. In such poems, the most memorable lines are those that express fierce indignation:

> Beating the drums
> my poetic voice
> proclaimed to all:
> those are unstained hands.
> Now,
> a slap in my face!

Along the same lines, the poet expresses, in another poem titled "By the River", his disappointment at the conflict between Tamil militant groups, resulting in mindless death.

> Folks
> do not build bridges
> with corpses
> to cross the river.

It is quite likely that Cheran's refusal to remain tied to any particular stance has given him a range and depth that sets him apart from many other poets.

Cheran's significance as a poet has been both documented and discussed more fully than perhaps any other contemporary Tamil poet. He is also perhaps the best known in India and internationally. Among Sri Lankan scholars, Sivathamby and Sivasegaram have written incisive essays on his poetry, while in Tamil Nadu Sundara Ramaswamy, Jeyamohan, Gnanakoothan, D Ravikumar, and M Ramasamy, among others, have drawn attention to his work. Although he started writing in the early 70s, he is in some ways the product of a time when the political scene was beginning to change rapidly, and the cultural forms of representation were becoming a crucial part of the transformation. In addition to being deeply concerned about politics and culture, his poetry was meant for a large readership, without necessarily jettisoning a commitment to a noticeable intellectual rigour. To put it differently, the distinctiveness of his poetry lies in his capacity to bring together the traditional and the modern, the lyrical and the intellectual. Even at its most abstract, the poetry retains the tone of oral delivery, while the various tropes insist on a complex train of thought. Cheran's poetry, in addition to being deeply contextual, forces the reader to read carefully and slowly. This could have something to do with his own training in the sciences, or his academic life as a sociologist, but the fact remains that the internal logic of his poems compels the reader to pay close attention to the working of language and metaphor.

Cheran began writing consistently at a time when students, particularly undergraduates, were deeply preoccupied with the rapid escalation of political conflict. Poetry was seen as an important way of reaching out to the people, and Cheran himself, having grown up with the notion of poetry as performance, was now able to harness this experience and mould it to the new context. His poetry was both recited and performed in towns and villages. And in these instances, passion and lyricism were as important as intellectual rigour. Cheran's poetry, in its performative aspect, needed to engage with people in a very direct manner. He is among a handful of poets who wrote many poems that were meant to be sung and performed and an equal number of poems that were deeply introspective and intellectually complex. The latter, in particular, are distinctly modernist and do not lend themselves easily to oral delivery. In them a number of graphic and disturbing images, not overtly connected to each other, are put together so that the overall effect on the reader is both diachronic and synchronic. These poems have a distinctly imagist and surreal quality to them. Through a process of defamiliarization they demonstrate a passionate commitment to political events and a skepticism about the danger of emotional excess.

For those who are familiar with the cultural and political context which form the backdrop to Cheran's poetry, a number of poems remain emphatically specific. A few poems, such as "The Second Sunrise" are intended to draw attention to certain events that are well known to everyone. In that sense, such poems are metonymic. Here the poet assumes the role of chronicler, speaking about a particular event in ways that are new and significant. Many other poems, however, are deliberately ambivalent. For the reader who has extensive knowledge of the political backdrop, these poems are about specific places and events. For others, the poems are sufficiently generalized to express the pervasive experience of pain, loss, and trauma. It is this capacity to maintain a balance between the specific and the general that has enabled Cheran's poems to remain relevant long after certain events have faded from collective memory. A poem such as "Glass Rain" reverberates at many levels, and while the Western reader and a Tamil reader might respond to the poem in very different ways, the chances are that both will recognize the trauma of entrapment and mass destruction.

Jeyamohan in an essay makes the observation that the poem about the burning of the Jaffna Public Library is among the best that Cheran has written (2008, 24-36). It is perhaps more true to say that such poems reflect the distinctiveness of Cheran's poetry and sets it apart from many others. These poems draw attention to a political context that is not always overt, but familiar to those who have some knowledge of the times. Often the references are quite specific to particular moments or events. The poet positions himself as an insider, very much like the informed reader. As the poem progresses, the particular event begins to shed light in very different ways. Layers of meaning begin to accumulate, changing the event through an imagination that moves across time and space. The poem itself becomes increasingly allusive until the specific and the general merge, and a particular moment is both fixed in time and timeless in its deeper meanings. As Jeyamohan implies, this is precisely why a poem about a particular time and place transcends its temporal boundaries to become a major work. There is tremendous irony and pathos in calling the burning of a major library a kind of sunrise. But the irony is deliberate. To call it a form of sunset would rob the poem of its urgency, resolve, and optimism.

Linking the specific to the general or the metonymic to the metaphoric often entails a number of challenges for the poet. In the first instance, the moment that occasions a particular poem engages the subjectivity of the poet, compelling him to write in ways that draw on certain images. In poems such as "By the River" which might well refer to the conflicts between two militant groups, the cluster of images draw on the landscape, the river, and nature, to emphasize specificity. But such conflicts are also reminiscent of other conflicts that are needlessly destructive, and in order to encapsulate them within the frame of the poem, the imagery becomes very different. Two levels thus coexist in Cheran's poetry, making him both a very local poet concerned with immediate realities and a modernist poet with a broad sweep. Tracking certain patterns of imagery is often a useful way of understanding the thematic links that run through Cheran's work.

Among the recurring tropes in his corpus, the sea appears time and again in various forms. It is not without significance that his very first poem was titled "Sea" when it appeared in 1975. His most recent collection is titled *Meendum Kadalukku* (Back to the Sea, 2005), published, coincidentally, soon after the Tsunami hit South Asia. For an island people, it is hardly surprising that the sea is important in both a literal and metaphoric sense. The sea provides freedom and security; it is a protection against outsiders, but it also alienates and makes people insular and vulnerable. The sea takes on a special significance as it embraces various forms of water—rivers, wells, tears, and so forth. His collected poems, published in 2000, has an equally interesting title: *Nee Ippozhuthu Irangum Aru* (The River You Now Step Into), implying the inevitability of change and movement. Writing in the 70s, the sea was benign:

> Evenings caressed by the night,
> the palmyrah leaves then
> lift their heads and sway,
> now the waves rise in
> the caress of the night
> the caress of the night. (2000, 24)

In the post-1983 phase, the imagery and the diction change:

> From this shore to the next,
> long, heat-carrying tubes,
> run across the bottom;
> the water torn apart,
> icebergs shattered
> the path they create
> day and night
> ships ply the sea. (2005, 25)

Between the tragedy of ethnic violence and the sorrow of exile, Cheran finds himself writing a poetry that combines restraint with a deep sense of commitment. In poems such as "Demonic Eyes" the contemporary political scene becomes the occasion for unrestrained satire. It is also multifaceted satire, looking inward and outward, speaking of the past but foretelling the future. It even invokes the notion of gender without becoming dogmatic in its stance. Cheran often alludes to the demonic and the supernatural to find a trope for the excesses that people face all the time. Often the imagery provides a sense of distance, while the rhythms retain that sense of familiarity. As Sivathamby says, quite rightly, "Cheran's poetry demonstrates how the new generation recognizes, responds to and understands the experiential changes in society" (2000, 101). Negotiating this change is as much about subject matter as it is about style and language. Often the shift in perspective, the movement from one voice to another may become a strategy for including multiple voices and perspectives. Cheran's struggle as a poet comes from the recognition that tradition is both an asset and an impediment. Working with a literary tradition that goes back to more than twenty centuries often entails drawing from a rich archive of poetic forms and linguistic diversity. If Cheran's poetry has a rich oral dimension it is because Tamil poetry has always incorporated an oral quality. For Cheran it is as important to draw from the past while defamiliarizing his poetry in order to make it both contemporary and original.

Cheran's first collection of poems is titled *Irandavathu Suriya Uthayam* (The Second Dawn). Ironically, the second dawn symbolizes the fire that engulfed the Jaffna Public Library when it was burned down in 1981. Since then, with each book, the title has a story to tell. These stories chart the poet's emotional story through tempestuous times, leading to exile in Canada. The imagination that captures these narratives is often quite startling in its capacity to accommodate the inhuman and the non-human. A severed leg or a demonic goddess can become the subject of his poems, but the language remains both grounded and strange at the same time. The reader is often swept along by the rhythm, the repetitions, the refrains, all of which suggest a certain familiarity between the poet and the reader. And yet the structure of the poem is deliberately allusive, moving across time and space, always implying layers of complex meaning.

In fact, in his critical writing he has advanced the very interesting notion that the social and cultural backdrop of the diaspora needs to be thought of not simply as nostalgia or exile, but as an extension of the *tinai* concept prevalent in Sangam poetry (Cheran 2007, 150-168). Inasmuch as the poetics of the Sangam age was dependent on particular aspects of landscape, so does the poetry of diaspora draw on the specificities of an alien landscape and its social practices. His notion of diaspora as self-sufficient space with its own norms and conventions allows for his poetry to acquire that sense of naturalness while being different. Thus a meeting between the poet and a First Nations elder is both unusual and predictable. Such poems maintain that balance between the unfamiliar and the familiar that is crucial to his poetry. Diaspora has been, for Cheran, a source of empowerment. While the yearning for "home" has not been in any way diminished by distance, diaspora has extended the range of his perception and shaped the trajectory of his poetry.

Cheran's displacement within the country and in Europe was often the result of escaping the wrath of different players in the political arena. In such circumstances, the poetry remained committed to the particular and the specific. It was hardly possible to be an activist and a poet without invoking the political events of the time. Pathos, outrage, and optimism are all inevitable subjective responses to the constant changes as one scenario gave way to another. Cheran's poems continue to engage us largely because the poems are shaped by an imagination that goes beyond the immediate. The widespread violence of 1983 might be the immediate context of a particular poem, but the I/eye that perceives the carnage focuses on a particular moment that in its insignificance suddenly takes on a human dimension that goes beyond the immediate moment. In a poem such as "Forgetting" the poet records in minute detail moments of horror as people are blown apart, but the most tragic moment is when a pot of rice is shattered, and a woman's children, hiding in the bushes, are denied their food. Understatement is a staple feature of Cheran's poetry. At the most intense moments, the diction gets pared down to essentials. The prose is simple, almost monosyllabic, but retains its powerful impact.

From the time he began writing three decades ago, Cheran has been concerned with the role of the poet in times of upheaval. In poems that were written in times when his own safety was in question, the poet expresses both the trauma of having to live in hiding and also the commitment to survive. Time and again, such poems assert the need for both awareness and distance. These are poems of fear and terror as the language offers a range of imagery that overturns a natural order:

> What will happen
> when I die and depart?
>
> If it happens to be dawn
> the moon will rise.
> . . . . .
> If it happens to be night
> the birds, woken from sleep,
> will sing.
>
> In the melody of that song
> The feathers of the lapwing will burn.

The poet must survive, and bear witness to the carnage around. Cheran's poetry is always conscious that it is all too easy to be swept away by the horror of the moment. But the poet is also the chronicler of the times and must struggle to preserve a sense of detachment:

> Unperturbed
> he writes his poem

Something of this uncertainty comes across in many of his self-reflexive poems in which he feels the need to reiterate his commitment to life and to his freedom to criticize. Even in his bleakest poems, there is a determination to live, to express his complex response to the violence around.

> let my pyre burn
> to shed a tiny light.
>
> From that light
> a song will appear.

Ideas of conflict, resistance, subversion, recuperation, fragmentation and dispersal keep appearing in various guises. The more recent poems are, in that sense, no different. But the telling has been always shaped by circumstance. In the aftermath of the violence of 2009, the poems are spare, devoid of profusion of imagery, but powerful nonetheless. The distance between his recent poems and his early poems in the 1970s is quite striking, and they indicate the impressive trajectory of a remarkable body of poetry. Derek Walcott ends his poem titled "Mass Man" with the following stanza:

> Upon your penitential morning.
> some skull must rub its memory with ashes,
> some mind must squat down howling in your dust,
> some hand must crawl and recollect your rubbish,
> someone must write your poems. (Walcott 31)

This is precisely what Cheran has done over a period of three decades.

South Asian Poetry in Canada: In Search of a Place

Arun Prabha Mukherjee

This article appeared originally in A Meeting of Streams *(TSAR Publications, 1985), and is the first serious consideration of the then emerging diversity of Canadian poetry.*

In their introduction to a special issue of *Canadian Ethnic Studies* devoted to the theme of "Ethnicity and Canadian Literature," the editors, commenting on the "predominantly Anglo-Gaelic or French character" of the official view of Canadian literature, ask:

> . . . where are the fictional remembrances of the Chinese, the Japanese, the Greeks, the Finns, the Ukrainians, to name only a few? (Kroetsch et al 1982, iv)

The special issue brings to surface "ethnic" writers whose work has not been accepted into the mainstream.

Canadian Ethnic Studies is not unique in arguing for a view of Canadian literature that is different from the received one. Several recent publishing events suggest the development of a real awareness in the intellectual circles of the pluralistic nature of Canadian society. *Canadian Literature* brought out a special issue on Caribbean writers in Canada in the winter of 1982, and the *Journal of Canadian Studies* published an issue on multiculturalism in the spring of 1982. One hopes that intellectual acts such as these will result in a rewriting of Canadian literary and cultural history. One may even look forward some day to a longer rejoinder to E J Pratt's "Towards the Last Spike" than F R Scott's short poem reprimanding Pratt for overlooking the role of the Chinese workers in building the transcontinental railroad.

A notable addition to this multicultural Canadian literature is the work of writers of South Asian origins.[1] These writers deserve to be acknowledged on the strength of numbers alone. Indeed, the number of South Asian writers active on the Canadian literary scene is quite astounding given the fact that South Asians, who are relatively new to Canada, account for less than 1 percent of the country's population. A very encouraging sign of the vitality of South Asian writing in Canada is the publication of journals like the *Toronto South Asian Review* and *Rupture*, which provide a forum for creative and critical endeavours. Unfortunately, however, only Michael Ondaatje has been officially recognized, and the rest remain virtually unknown. One other writer, Bharati Mukherjee, gained some notoriety with her farewell-to-Canada article in *Saturday Night*.

In this article I intend to comment on the work of South Asian poets in Canada. Apart from Ondaatje, who needs no introduction, Himani Bannerji, Krisantha Sri Bhaggiyadatta, Rienzi Crusz, Cyril Dabydeen, Lakshmi Gill, Reshard Gool, Arnold Itwaru, Surjeet Kalsey, Suniti Namjoshi, S Padmanab, Uma Parameswaran, and Asoka Weerasinghe have all had at least one collection of their poems published. Indeed, most of them have published more than one collection.

Although these poets admittedly come from different parts of the globe—for example, Guyana, India, the Philippines and Sri Lanka—a number of links tie them to one another. There is the ancestral link to the Indian subcontinent that gives common racial features to South Asians and makes them recognizable as a visible minority. Also, there are several cultural practices that South Asians continue to share, however distant their connection to the Indian subcontinent may be. Finally, there is the colonial experience that originally scattered South Asians to all parts of the world.

These historical linkages emerge as some identifiable patterns in the subject matter as well as the technique of South Asian poetry. The recurrence of these patterns in the work of South Asian poets, and their relative unimportance in the work of other Canadian poets, makes South Asian poetry highly interesting as a literary phenomenon both in terms of its new perspective on Canadian society and its rather unconventional relationship with the dominant literary tradition. The South Asian poet may be said to possess that double vision which comes only when one is alienated from the dominant group: the condition of writers as diverse as Henry James, Theodore Dreiser, Richard Wright, and Salman Rushdie. This outsider is painfully aware of the contradictions that the cement of a homogeneous ideology carefully conceals from a full-fledged member of the dominant group. Consequently, South Asian poets write less about man's response to nature, the woes of age and death, the joys and pains of sexual love, and other such staples of poets through the ages, and more about racism, poverty, discrimination, colonial exploitation, imperialism, and ideological domination. Although some South Asian poets do write on these perennial subjects, their strength as well as their preoccupations are accounted for, I believe, in terms of their otherness and visibility.[2]

The otherness of South Asian poets means that they have come to Canada, in Dabydeen's words, "mudbound in memory" (1979, 64). These poets, coming from countries that have only recently emerged from colonial domination and are plagued by poverty and political violence, continue to write about their places of origin. Unlike other immigrant poetry, however, South Asian poetry does not indulge in nostalgia or in what the editors of the aforementioned special issue of *Canadian Ethnic Studies* termed "ethnic genealogy." Instead of a romanticization of the lost Eden—and one does come across some of that as well—South Asian poetry attempts to draw the attention of the Canadian reader to the misery of poverty:

> loving you,
> I think of twisted, leprous hands,
> rains laying waste the year's harvest
> people shooting each other off
> in war
> or by accident.
>
> You think I have wandered off
> into a private land of pleasure,

leaving you lonely
in your turbulence.

But love,
I will join you,
my lust a trifle late perhaps,
when I have rebuilt cities
and caused children
to be born perfect
in a loving world,

as you lie thinking,
how long will he take. (Padmanab 1977, 26)

Here it is interesting to note that the South Asian poet does not remain confined by national boundaries but seems to identify with the entire Third World, reflecting the sense of solidarity the Third World countries have come to share because of their history. Thus, Himani Bannerji from India writes poems on Victor Jara and Salvadore Allende, and Asoka Weerasinghe, a Sri Lankan poet, writes about the misery of the war-torn Sahelia:

Life wrapped by naked skin
moves feebly south,
the salivary glands
parched by desiccation
and each mouth
open to gobble the hot air.
They pass neo-middens
of man, bird and mammal,
smoking under the hot sun
all scaled and bare,
where there are no flowers to bear
the lily-smell of death,
of an African "quality of life." (Weerasinghe 1976, 27)

It is apparent from the above examples that South Asian poetry abounds in images of violence, suffering, and death. In a society of plenty where obesity happens to be a national problem, a preoccupation with malnourished and diseased forms may sound distant and jarring. The South Asian poet, therefore, has to make sure that his poetry is firmly bound to the Canadian context. To ensure this, he often so structures his poems as to join the two realms of his experience in a meaningful way. Some of the devices he uses are letters home that talk about Canada to a person who is a stranger to Canadian ways; physical and spiritual journeys that, apart from articulating the poet's own experience as an immigrant, also bring in references to the historical journeys of the past, such as those of the *Komagata Maru* and the indentured labourers; contrasts of season—where Canadian winter often symbolizes the death of poetic inspiration as well as the lack of friendliness on the part of the host society; and dreams joining the poet's life at home with existence here as seen in his psychic life. This poem by Arnold Itwaru, for example, contrasts the two realms through the conjunctions which only dreams provide:

> Half-formed, malformed, they are there in my sleep,
> they are there when I awake. Explosions of
> clocks and faces, of flesh and bone. I run
> from them but they erupt before me. I see
> them, but what are they? I've tried to forget
> them, to tell myself I'm okay, you're okay,
> we're all okay, I've tried to reason
> them out of existence. . . .
>
> . . . behind the pages, the pictures, the
> streets, children eat adults, adults eat
> children, they all eat garbage, morsel to
> morsel, blood for blood, spectres, caricatures,
> skeletons, corpses, tumescent in endless
> oceans (Itwaru 1981, 55)

Whereas the dream structure of the poem allows the poet to bring in experiences so radically alien to Canadian life, his mocking reference to the bestseller *I'm OK, You're OK* effectively contrasts the two worlds. With remarkable economy, the title of the bestseller underlines the poet's disappointment with the affluent West's attitude to the developing countries. The poem, while mocking the narcissism of the individualistic philosophy propounded in the book, shows that the problems it deals with are those of affluence. Thus, in counterpointing itself against an ironic allusion, the poem gains multiplicity of meaning and resonance.

A number of South Asian poets use this strategy of ironic contrast. This they bring to bear on the poem through an allusion to a shibboleth of the dominant culture. The following poem by Bhaggiyadatta is a good example:

> we came
> in 747s
> to sink
> to the bottom
> of the upheld mosaic:
> to push mailcarts
> ("beaverbrook started this way you know")
> . . . .
> the natives say it's initiation
> they did it to the irish
> the italian the gay
> but we are better
> niggers
> we take shit with
> a smile
> and a colour tv. (Bhaggiyadatta 1981, 9-10)

Bhaggiyadatta mocks the equalitarian pretensions of the mosaic metaphor as well as the favourite myth of North American capitalism: that of the self-made man. This satirical sparring against the powers that be stands in contrast to the thematic concerns of much recent "mainstream" Canadian poetry whose mood remains largely neoromantic. Unlike the self-enclosed, meditative poetic mode so popular among modern Anglo-Canadian poets, the South Asian poetic mode is one of ironic relationships. The outside world is brought into the poem to provide resonances and contrasts, most of them bitterly ironic. The poems repeatedly confront and challenge social policy. Sometimes, as in Bannerji's "Terror," the note is extremely dark. This poem gives voice to the suppressed rage as well as the terror that South Asian immigrants feel under the oppression of hate messages on telephone, broken window panes, and physical and verbal assaults. The irony in the poem is deepened by Bannerji's use of symbols derived from history and contemporary reality.

The symbolism of King George's equestrian statue in Queen's Park in Toronto arises from the fact that it was brought to Canada from India after the latter decided to discard all visual reminders of its colonial masters. For this South Asian poet, then, the statue is not merely a nice backdrop for a photograph but a painful reminder of her past and her differences with the Canadian society:

> I think of my daughter, I grow afraid, I see designs against her deep-set into their concrete structures or embossed into their Education Act. The blue of the sky, the gold of the sun, becomes an Aryan-eyed blonde and her spiked heels dig into my bowels. (Bannerji 1982, 25)

The "Aryan-eyed blonde" with "her spiked heels" becomes representative of contemporary Canadian society. The figure is based on an actual woman, a member of the Ku Klux Klan, who used to march on the Toronto streets most frequented by South Asians in the company of KKK men, taunting, threatening, and terrorizing the city's visible minorities.

Judging from the tone and the subject matter of South Asian poetry, it can be said that the South Asian consciousness is out of harmony with the accepted beliefs and practices of the host society. This sense of being out of step results at times in bitter anger, as in Bannerji and Bhaggiyadatta, and at other times in playful mockery, as in Rienzi Crusz's "The Sun-Man's Poetic Five Ways":

> Who, brown and strolling
> down a Toronto street,
> came up against these black vinyl jackets
> with mouths hurling their paki paki words like knives;
> froze, then quickly thawed to his notebook:
> "Color of offenders' eyes: hazel, blue, blue.
> Hair: All long, like Jesus, down the nape.
> Estimated educational background: TV's *Police Story*,
> starring Angie Dickinson.
> Home address: Paradise Blvd., Toronto.
> Possible motives: Kicks.
> So much poetry in the trajectory of crow sounds." (Crusz 1982, 54)

Even though the poem shows a tremendous sense of restraint in the poet's refusal to let his hurt show, the purpose is identical to Bannerji's in "Terror." The question implied is, how can a society that prides itself in its democratic institutions allow the existence of such injustices? The perversion of the message of Jesus and the emergence of the new "heroes" casually hint at the moral decay threatening this society.

Perhaps only the sufferer can tell where the shoe pinches. Thus, although "mainstream" Canadian poetry does not treat racism as an important subject matter, it is one of the predominant concerns of South Asian poetry. This short poem of Lakshmi Gill is very suggestive in its hesitant tone and its reference to the persona's colour:

> blue ice
> (O my Canada)
> can I call
> you mine
> foreign sad
> brown that
> I am (Gill 1972, 6)

Yet another aspect of the immigrant experience for the South Asian poet is that of being dislocated in terms of social and economic class. Even an immigrant from an affluent background might have to undergo the humiliation of becoming "lower class." As a result, immigrant writing in general is more class-conscious. To cite again from the editorial of *Canadian Ethnic Studies*: "By portraying the immigrant and ethnic experience, which has often been lived in a working-class milieu, 'ethnic' writers have provided a thematic perspective that has largely been missing at the centre of Canadian literature which, academic and elitist, has given little space to the drama of class struggle and its individual tragedies" (Kroetsch et al, v). The South Asian poet, of necessity, writes about his treatment at the hands of landlords and immigration officials, racist graffiti in public washrooms, and his experiences at the workplace:

> FACE IT THERE'S AN ILLEGAL
> IMMIGRANT
> HIDING IN YOUR HOUSE
> HIDING IN YOU
> TRYING TO GET OUT!
> . . . .

TRYING TO GET IN
ON YOUR AFFLUENT FANTASIES
AND FIFTY-CENT FEARS

(BUSINESSMEN CUSTOMS OFFICIALS
DARK GLASSES INDUSTRIAL AVIATION
POLICEMEN ILLEGAL BACHELORETTES
SWEATSHOP KEEPERS INFORMATION CANADA
SAYS
"YOU CAN'T GET THEIR SMELL OFF THE WALLS"
(Bhaggiyadatta 1981, 23)

Sukhwant Hundal's "A Letter to a Friend" comments on the persona's life in Canada in the context of the mythical images of the Western world's prosperity that circulate in the developing societies:

You might have imagined me
sitting in a chair surrounded by machines,
touch-pushing switches with my fingers . . .

How can I tell you—when pulling
the four-by-twelve-by-twenty-two boards
how they drag my body
and sap its strength;
or when holding in my hand a broom
taller than myself
I spick and span the floor,
I am reminded of the good old college days
when we used to rebuke the janitor
for blowing dust while brooming the floor. (1983, 77)

Ironically, instead of sending this letter, which lets his friend in India know "the truth," the persona writes another letter "full of colourful lies," which hides how his "self-esteem falls apart into dust" (Hundal, 77-78).

The poem is a poignant comment on the fragility of the immigrant's psyche, battered as it is by individual and institutionalized racism. It is not only the oppressive external forces that the South Asian poet writes about, however. The poems of Uma Parameswaran give vent to another kind of fragmentation of the South Asian's sense of identity. Parameswaran writes about the conflicts present within the family itself. While this, again, is a subject common to immigrant poetry in general, the matter is further complicated for the South Asian poet by the fact that South Asian children are precluded by their skin colour from merging unobtrusively into the society at large. Written in the form of a child's monologue addressed to his mother, this poem by Parameswaran brings to light the self-hatred of a nonwhite child confronted by a society unwilling to respect his "differentness":

> Ma, you think you could change my name
> To Jim or David or something?
> . . . .
> When the snow comes, Ma
> I'll get less brown won't I?
> It would be nice to be white,
> more like everyone else
> you know? (Parameswaran 1990, 15)

Though the subject is extremely painful, the irony is deliberately muted. The appeal to the Canadian reader to do something about the state of affairs is made very deviously. Nonetheless, the poem is highly effective in its understatement.

Much of South Asian Canadian poetry, like this poem, bears the character of a rhetorical appeal, even when it does not address the reader directly. Ranging through various levels of irony, it insists on confronting the reader with the contradictions between the society's preaching and practice. Its achievement can be defined, in Kenneth Burke's terms, as providing us with a "perspective by incongruity." A good writer, Burke says, provides new insights by "violating the 'proprieties' of the word in its previous linkages" (1935, 90). As must be clear from the examples quoted thus far, South Asian Canadian poetry is, above all, a violation of proprieties. In its constant insistence on questioning the rules of the game, as it were, it makes us aware of the ludicrousness of several solemn ceremonies. Take, for example, Suniti Namjoshi's "Poem Against Poets," which shrewdly exposes the shortcomings of Western patriarchal aesthetic norms:

> I fall upon the thorns of life
>   I weep, I bleed
> but to what Purpose?

There was once a poet
who thought she was a nightingale,
and another
who thought she was a rose—
charming perhaps,
able certainly, having found at least
a way to cope.
Would the nightingale's entrails
have been more powerful
(as emblematic objects)
laid out on the floor
of a room that you came to, and then
withdrew from,
startled and amazed?
Oh the rose is bloodless,
she is white with pain;
and Philomel wails
in the woods again.
But there are the other
more ordinary animals.
They are not literary.
They own their pain. (1990, 62)

The poem effectively points out the reasons many Third World writers feel so alienated from the Western literary traditions, even though they write in languages bequeathed to them by the colonial powers. Closer to home, it makes us aware of the structuralist-formalist stance of the literary criticism, so much in vogue in Canada, which dwells on images and symbols and other aspects of technique while disregarding the ideological and sociological aspects of literature. It also brings out the insularity of our departments of literature, which rarely tread outside the European literary tradition.

Himani Bannerji's "A Savage Aesthetic," a translation of a Bengali poem by Manabendra Bandopadhyay, makes a similar point. The poem is constructed in two parts. The first half of the poem is a lecture in a poetry class while the second half is the poet's rejoinder. The poem brings out the ideological stance of an aesthetic that prides itself in its objectivity:

"Remember, poetry too is architecture

> *all else is redundant except the form, the style—*
> *what you call—the texture."*
>
> . . . .
>
> . . . and so the poetry class unending.
> Always the same. Sharp, academic
> an exhibition of smug narcissism. Full of apt
> and self-conscious quotations, allusions and message
> in a voice that plays with a joke or two
> calculating, avoiding emotional excess.
> So stands this hour of aesthetics, an exact reflection,
> of the confidence of the glass and concrete phallus
> that arises on an erased slum or broken shanty town. (1982, 46-47)

Such poems reflect the disillusionment of the South Asian poets with their Western literary training. For while their poetic strategies show their familiarity with it, their poems are really parodies of the dominant modes.

The South Asian poets invert Western myths for ironic purposes instead of using them seriously in the way Canadian mythopoeic poets like Jay MacPherson do, for instance. In "Lady Icarus," Dabydeen applies the myth to the story of Maria, an aspiring immigrant from Equador who fell to her death when trying to escape from detention by immigration authorities (1977, 16). Suniti Namjoshi's "Philomel" points out an aspect of the myth thus far unexplored:

> She had her tongue ripped out, and then she sang / down through the centuries. So that it seems only / fitting that the art she practices should be art for / art's sake, and never spelt out, no—never reduced / to its mere message—that would appal. (Tereus raped Philomela and cut out her tongue in / order to silence her. She was then transformed into / the "poetic" nightingale that sings so sweetly through Western tradition.) (1981, 102)

The inversion of Western myths, the use of ironic forms, the retorts to Western writers and critics, all point out the South Asian poets' sense of the unsuitability of the Western literary tradition for their purposes. Itwaru, for example, clears out his territory by removing the familiar landmarks that the Western reader takes for granted:

> NOTICE
>
> ENTER THIS WILDERNESS AT YOUR OWN RISK. THERE ARE / NO VIRGILS HERE. BEATRICE AWAITS NOWHERE. THERE / ARE CANOEISTS, BUT YOU WILL FIND NO CHARON.
>
> YOU / SHOULD BE WARNED THAT THE RIVERS ARE POISONOUS. / OTHER THAN YOU THERE ARE NO DANGEROUS ANIMALS. (Itwaru 1981, 54)

Itwaru, like so many modern Third World poets, declares that the idiom of Western poetry is insufficient for him. The long tradition that Western poets rely on in creating their meaning is discarded as so much jetsam. This has to be done because the tradition does not represent the history of a Third World poet like Itwaru. Of course, the poet discards it only symbolically. The things to be rejected have to be named if others are to understand this act of rebellion. Conventions have to be used if only in order to be stood on their head.

These constant inversions show how difficult the task of the South Asian poet actually is when compared with that of a writer who feels at home in his tradition. Salman Rushdie has described it in his novel *Shame* while expressing his frustration about rendering concepts of a culture in a foreign tongue that has no equivalents for them:

> This word: "shame." No, I must write it in its original form, not in this peculiar language tainted by wrong concepts and the accumulated detritus of its owners' unrepented past, this Angrezi in which I am forced to write, and so for ever alter what is written . . . .
>
> *Sharam*, that's the word. For which this paltry "shame" is a wholly inadequate translation. . . . A short word, but one containing encyclopaedias of nuance. (1983, 38-39)

Raja Rao, the celebrated Indian novelist, made the same point in 1937 while describing his efforts to tell a story from "the contemporary annals" of his village: "the telling has not been easy. One has to convey in a language that is not one's own the spirit that is one's own" (v). The titles of the works of South Asian poets indicate the nature of the difficulties they face in communicating their vision here in Canada; titles like *A Separate Sky, Distances, Shattered Songs*, and *Rupture* declare their sense of working against the current.

When the South Asian poet inverts accepted meanings, he is at least using a familiar idiom, though in a different key. But as one cannot remain in a state of perpetual reaction, the South Asian poet invents his own language. The difficulties of this task are well outlined in Dabydeen's "For the Sun Man," a poem addressed to fellow South Asian poet Rienzi Crusz. The poet commends Crusz for his ability to "pluck parables / from the Buddha's / core" while he himself, "being so much / like the West," is suffering from a loss of creativity. The poem states the need for creating new metaphors as the old ones no longer work (Dabydeen 1982, 51). The "Sun Man" the poem's title refers to is Crusz's mythic persona and occurs in several of his poems. The persona allows Crusz to amalgamate the two segments of his life in a meaningful way while it works as a readily available device with which to build further.

A number of poets "pluck parables" from their South Asian past. Surjeet Kalsey's "Siddhartha Does Penance Again" (1983) compares the journey of a modern-day immigrant to that of the Buddha leaving home in his search for enlightenment. The poem plays with the difference between the two Siddharthas and the nature of their journeys. Suniti Namjoshi's *Feminist Fables* borrows its form from the ancient Indian tales of the *Pancatantra*. Using tales from the *Pancatantra* as well as from nursery rhymes, classical mythology, and the *Arabian Nights*, Namjoshi makes satirical comments on the place of women in modern society. It is a highly original work that is complex without becoming inaccessible.

Perhaps, for an uninitiated reader who has had no cross-cultural experience, the use of such resources will be difficult to comprehend. However, the South Asian poet is compelled to use them as nothing else can be substituted in their place. Uma Parameswaran's "Ganga Jal" demonstrates the importance of myth and ritual for poetry as well as the fact that language is not merely grammar and syntax but buried culture. For "Ganga jal" is a phrase that stirs some very profound emotions in a Hindu mind. It means the water of the holy river Ganga, which is needed in Hindu homes to perform several sacraments related to birth, initiation, and death. Ganga water is poured into the mouth of a dying person, and after cremation the ashes of Hindus are strewn in the river. Every believing Hindu, hence, keeps at least a bottle of Ganga water at home. Given this context, the reader realizes by the end of the first stanza that the poem is about imminent death:

> I heard him come in the door
> And straight to the kitchen.
> He had snowflakes in his hair
> And his face was white as any neighbour's
> All blood from it in his burning eyes
> His boots formed an instant puddle
> As he stood at the kitchen door.
>
> Gangajal, he said, I need Gangajal. (Parameswaran 1990, 75-77)

The poem captures a very intimate aspect of South Asian life in Canada. The household gods, the container of Ganga jal, the rituals of birth and death: who else will write about these aspects of South Asian experience except a South Asian poet? The poem is extremely moving as it dramatically renders the anguish of dying so far away from one's home and traditions. However, alien as its allusions are to Canadian readers, it is doubtful if it would have the same impact on a person unacquainted with the Indian ethos.

No doubt, a poetry that contains unfamiliar names of poets, gods, historical figures, Third World personalities, inversions of conventional poetic idiom, and, at times, rhythms and diction unfamiliar to the North American ear can seem obscure. However, if literature were taught in a multicultural context, as a means of promoting an understanding of the dependency of literature on culture, tradition, and history, South Asian poetry in Canada could serve as a useful means of comparison. It could then provide a valuable tool for teachers of literature in introducing their students to ways of apprehending the world that are different from those they have been brought up with. Ioan Davies's remarks about the poetry of Bannerji and Itwaru can be applied to the contribution of the South Asian poets in general: "Their uniqueness is that they are representatives of a generation of writers in Canada who are not part of the mainstream of our literature." Their works, Davies goes on to say, are "the expressions of an otherness against a hegemony in which the terms of reference are dictated by the preoccupations of those who have established themselves as the centre-pieces of a dominating culture" (1982, 34). The act of making the dominating culture self-conscious is in itself a contribution that should allot South Asian poetry, along with the literature of other racial and ethnic minorities in Canada, an important niche in Canadian literature.

Notes

Fielding Ondaatje: A Brief Look at the "Canadian" Response

1. Hereafter referred to as *Running.*

2. It is no accident that I focus primarily on the critical climate that emerged out of Toronto from the 1980s onward, since it provides a rather unique concentration of Ondaatje critics (Canadian, Sri Lankan diasporic and otherwise) within a 30 mile radius.

3. For example, this enables Hutcheon to translate "Karapotha," cockroach, as "beetles that crawl over the land but see nothing," p. 308. Given the fact that the cockroach, as a derogatory descriptor of the Burger people, has a very specific cultural connotation in the Sri Lankan context (which Ondaatje is aware of) Hutcheon's analysis could benefit with an accurate translation of the word.

4. Writing on *Running*, Mukherjee states: "In an earlier essay, I have criticized the book and its reviewer for 'Exoticizing.' I was quite pleased to come across a review by a Sri Lankan critic [Ismail] who had similar reactions" (73).

5. Once again, I stress the importance of reading such contextual information in the full complexity it affords. There are very few successful studies of the Burghers that capture the particular intricacies of their status in pre and post-Independence Sri Lanka. The many essays by Ernest MacIntyre, or Raheem, in Roberts and Colin-Thome's *People inbetween* (1989) are excellent contemporaneous resources in this aspect. However, Sugunasiri's approach suggests an apparent disregard for scholarly analyses on socio-historical moments in Sri Lanka. When the critic has appointed himself as historian, no other source is deemed relevant.

6. MacIntyre provides a pithy overview of the plight of the Burghers in "Outside of Time: Running in the Family," *Spider Blues*, p. 315.

7. In *Running* a distinct sense of fracture and dislocation is apparent enough in the narrator's anguished reference to Lear: "give the word" (162). Just eight years after Sugunasiri's essay appeared, Ondaatje published *Handwriting* in which we

find one of the clearest examples of his own sheathed response to the trauma of dislocation: "The last Sinhala word I lost / was vatura" (50).

8. Sugunasiri hails Asoka Weerasinghe as a superior Sri Lankan diasporic poet because his voice appears to capture a Sinhala poetics in English. Once again, we encounter a particular monolithic reading of the "Sri Lankan diasporic poet" that is primarily Sinhala and precludes articulation of the racial and cultural experiences of the Tamils, Burghers and people of mixed descent who, ironically, make up the majority in Sri Lankan diasporas around the world and in Canada. See Sugunasiri, "Sri Lankan Poets," pp. 69-70.

9. In fact, although Ismail's essay was written during his time at the University of Peradeniya, Sri Lanka, both Qadri Ismail and Yasmine Gooneratne are diasporic critics living and working in America and Australia.

10. Sugunasiri does not even attempt this critical dialogue, assuming that his personal understanding of the post-Independence Sinhala cultural revival is sufficient background for the task at hand. See Sugunasiri, "Sri Lankan Poets," pp. 66-67.

11. As Gamini Seneviratne reminds us, in a culture of iniquity the very words that inscribe guilt are hollow: "Let us speak of guilt. / A fashionable word. / A word made resonant with a passion / of the 'I accuse!' kind" (33).

12. This was to shift somewhat in the response to *Anil's Ghost* (2000). See Chelva Kanaganayakam, "In Defense of *Anil's Ghost*,"; and Marlene Goldman, "Representations of Buddhism in Michael Ondaatje's *Anil's Ghost*."

Caliban's Voice

1. Clarke's poetry merits commenting on because it uses photography from the archives of Black Nova Scotia to add perspective to the poetry as well as to show the continuity between his poetry and the communal experiences that engender it. Moreover each of the thirteen poems comprising the first section of *Saltwater Spirituals and Deeper Blues*, "Soul Songs," bears the title of a Black Nova Scotian church. In this regard both he and Philip are interested in showing how the word is distilled from, and perhaps limited by, the larger world.

2. See George Lamming, "A Monster, a Child, a Slave," in *The Pleasures of Exile* (London: Allison & Busby [1960], 1984), 95-117; Kofi Awoonor, "Caliban Answers Prospero: The Dialogue between Western and African Literature," in *Obsidian: Black Literature in Review* 7 (2 & 3) (Spring 1982), 75-97; Max Dorsinville, *Caliban without Prospero* (Erin, Ontario: Porcepic Press, 1974), 9-17. All three theorists agree that Caliban, loosely defined as citizens of those countries the Occident terms the "Third World," occupies the unenviable position of rectifying the lies that Europeans—Prospero—have told. Dorsinville sees Caliban and Prospero as halves of the same dialectic, with Caliban's role being to remove the shadow Prospero has cast over him (15). Awoonor, more pessimistic, sees Caliban, the "Third World" writer, trapped for a very long time within the periphery of Prospero's heinous propaganda: "It is when he exhausts [Prospero's] arguments, and the other perhaps finally becomes silent that the ["Third World"] writer may then begin to

look at himself. But inevitably, that look, touched by history, shall remain cast and defined in the other's image" (97). Lamming's position is extremely complex for it focuses on the enriching as well as the damning aspect of Prospero's "gift," and looks to the future for some sort of resolution out of the slave-master relationship that the "gift" of language helps to consolidate (109-110).

3. I use the term "conjure" in its sense of sorcery. If we accept that Prospero employing the "sorcery" from his books controlled Caliban, one must understand Caliban's undoing of those spells as a counter-sorcery: a counter-conjure.

4. The essays of Hoyt Fuller, Larry Neal, Ron Karenga, Don Lee, John Oliver Killens, et al in *The Black Aesthetic*, edited by Addison Gayle, Jr (Garden City, NY: Doubleday Anchor Books, 1972) have a great deal to say about the function of the African American writer in providing African Americans with radically different visions of self-liberation from those proffered by White America and Black Integrationists.

5. See Walcott's "The Muse of History, (2)." John Hearne argues that the creole languages of the Caribbean are inadequate for presenting complex reality (see his interview with Horace Goddard (36-38)). See this author's interview with Earl Lovelace, "From 'Freedom' to 'Liberation'" (19). See Chamoiseau's argument in *Lettres créoles* (171-205), that the models for a veritable Caribbean literature are to be found in the techiques of the oral storyteller.

Diasporic Violences, Uneasy Friendships, and Hiromi Goto's *The Kappa Child*

1. Not all Japanese Canadians and Japanese Americans co-operated with their governments' attempts to relocate them. As Roy Miki documents in his important work on the Japanese-Canadian redress movement, many protested the injustice of the government's actions. He cites the Nisei Mass Evacuation Group, mostly Nisei men, "who protested the federal government's policy of breaking up the family unit," as an example of resistance by Japanese Canadians (58).

2. In sharp contrast with the father's ahistorical method of growing rice, Blackfoot ways of growing tobacco involve rituals that incorporate historical and mythical elements: "While they're away, they must camp in four different places of increasing distances from the garden while mythical 'little people' tend to the crop. 'Some say the seeds are the dwarf people,' wrote Wissler. 'No one must ever try to see the little people for if you do you will die.' At the fourth campsite, the women make tiny moccasins about five centimetres long and bags of food about seven centimetres long and put them out for the little people. The group then spends the rest of the summer hunting and gathering" (Chandler 35-6). These tobacco rituals and farming practices provide a way of seeing the geography of Alberta in deeply historical terms and as requiring balance amongst multiple kinds of forces: "As well as the mythical bringing of the original tobacco seed, the beaver and its aquatic habits played a leading role in ensuring the success of the crop by imparting information crucial for timing and locating tobacco" (Chandler 36).

3. This linking of Santa and Naapi draws on Eldon Yellowhorn's reading of

Santa as an appropriation of Naapi.

4. I thank Deanna Reder for making this astute observation. Given the multiple ways that the Indian Act excluded many from holding status, and Bill C-31, the Act that amended the former one and restored status to people such as those whose parents were not married, it is entirely possible that Gerald would have had no legal right to live on his father's reserve.

5. Judging by the narrator's viewing of the "last total eclipse of the twentieth century," which took place in September 1996, the novel seems to span a period that runs roughly from the mid-1960s to mid-1970s, and on until November 1996 (119).

Austin Clarke's Poetic Turn

1. Personal communication.

2. The Toronto trilogy includes *The Meeting Point* (1967), *Storm of Fortune* (1973) and *The Bigger Light* (1975).

3. *The Polished Hoe* won both the Scotiabank Giller Prize (2002) and the Commonwealth Prize for Literature (2003).

4. Various aspects of *Where the Sun Shines Best* echo *More*: Idora's apartment is also situated there; she remarks on the restricted vision her basement windows afford her, and the poet's cry to the black reservist, "Where is your dignity?" echoes that of Idora to the black man she disturbs rummaging through the garbage. The differences between her concerns and that of the poet illustrate what Brand calls poetry's diacritical power.

In Times of Upheaval: Cheran's Poetic Trajectory

1. Translation mine.

2. Cheran's publications include *Irandavathu Suriya Uthayam* (1983), *Yaman* (1984), *Kaanal Vari* (1989), *Elumbu Koodukalin Urvalam* (1990), and *Erithu Kondirukkum Neram* (1993). For his collected poems, see, A Yesurasa, R Cheran, *Nee Ippozhuthu Irangum Aaru* (Nagercoil, Tamil Nadu: Kalachuvadu, 2000). His most recent collection is titled *Meendum Kadalukku* (2005).

South Asian Poetry in Canada: In Search of a Place

1. The term South Asian is applied to denote immigrants who either have come to Canada directly from the Indian subcontinent (ie India, Pakistan, Bangladesh, and Sri Lanka) or have ancestral links with the subcontinent. Thus, many Caribbean immigrants to Canada are descendants of indentured labourers from northern India who were lured there by the British in the nineteenth century.

2. Insofar as Michael Ondaatje's work does not speak of his otherness and visibility, he is excluded from this article. Elsewhere I have commented on these omissions in his work.

References

Fielding Ondaatje: A Brief Look at the "Canadian" Response

Chamberlin, JE. "Let There be Commerce Between Us: The Poetry of Michael Ondaatje." *Spider Blues*, edited by Sam Solecki. Véhicule P, 1985.

Goldman, Marlene. "Representations of Buddhism in Michael Ondaatje's Anil's Ghost." *Comparative Cultural Studies and Michael Ondaatje's Writing*, edited by Steven Téotéosy de Zepetnek. Purdue UP, 2005.

Hutcheon, Linda. "Running in the Family: The Postmodernist Challenge." *Spider Blues*, edited by Sam Solecki. Véhicule P, 1985.

Ismail, Qadri. *Kaduwa*, 1, 1983.

Kanaganayakam, Chelva. "A Trick with a Glass: Michael Ondaatje's South Asian Connection." *Canadian Literature*, 132, 1992.

———. "In Defense of Anil's Ghost." *Ariel*, 37.1, 2006.

MacIntyre, Ernest. "Outside of Time: Running in the Family." *Spider Blues*, edited by Sam Solecki. Véhicule P, 1985.

Mount, Nick. "The Canlit Boom of the 1960s." Second Annual Katz Lecture, University of Toronto, 2010.

Mukherjee, Arun. "The Sri Lankan Poets in Canada: An Alternative View." *Towards an Aesthetic of Opposition*, William Wallace, 1988.

Ondaatje, Michael. *Handwriting*. Bloomsbury, 1999.

———. *Rat Jelly*. Coach House Books, 1973.

———. *Running in the Family*. Maclelland and Stewart, 1982.

———. *The Collected Works of Billy The Kid*. House of Anansi, 1970.

———. *The Dainty Monsters*. Coach House Books, 1967.

———. *There's a Trick with a Knife I'm Learning to Do*. McClelland and Stewart, 1979

Seneviratne, Gamini. "Of Guilt." *Navasilu*, edited by SW Perera. English Association of Sri Lanka, 1998.

Sugunasiri, Suwanda HJ. "'Sri Lankan Canadian Poets': The Bourgeoisie that Fled the Revolution." *Canadian Literature*, 132, 1992.

Caliban's Voice

Awoonor, Kofi. "Caliban Answers Prospero: The Dialogue between Western and African Literature." *Obsidian: Black Literature in Review* 7, (2-3), Spring 1982.

Baker, Houston A. *The Journey Back: Issues in Black Literature and Criticism*. University of Chicago Press, 1980.

Bakhtin, Mikhail. In Tzvetan Todorov. *Mikhail Bakhtin: The Dialogical Principle*. Translated by Wlad Godzich. University of Minnesota Press, 1984.

Barthes, Roland. *Writing Degree Zero*. Translated by Annette Lavers and Colin Smith. Noonday press, 1967.

Brathwaite, Edward K. *Folk Culture of the Slaves in Jamaica*. New Beacon Books, 1981.

Brown, Dee. *Bury My Heart at Wounded Knee: An Indian History of the American West*. Henry Holt & Company, 1970.

Chamoiseau, Patrick and Raphaël Confiant. *Lettres créoles:Tracées antillaises et continentales de la littérature*, 1635-1975. Hatier: 1991.

Clarke, George E. *Saltwater Spirituals and Deeper Blues*. Nova Scotia: Pottersfield Press, 1983.

Dorsinville, Max. *Caliban Without Prospero*. Porcepic Press, 1974.

Du Bois, William E B. *The Souls of Black Folk*. 1903. In Three Negro Classics, edited by John Hope Franklin. Avon Books, 1965.

Fanon, Frantz. *Black Skin, White Masks*. Grove Press, 1967

Gayle, Addison, Jr, editor. *The Black Aesthetic*. Anchor Books, 1972.

Glissant, Edouard. *Poétique de la Relation*. Gallimard, 1990.

Grier, William and Price Cobb. *Black Rage*. Bantam, 1968.

Hearne, John. Interview with Horace Goddard. In *A Common Tongue: Interviews with Cecil Abrahams, John Agard, John Hearne, Wole Soyinka*, edited by Horace Goddard. Afo, 1987.

Jung, Carl G. *The Undiscovered Self*. Translated by R F C Hull. Mentor Books, 1958.

Lamming, George. *The Pleasures of Exile*. Allison and Busby, 1960 [1984].

Lovelace, Earl. "From 'Freedom' to 'Liberation': Interview with H Nigel Thomas." *World Literature Written in English* 31 (1), Spring 1991.

Philip, Marlene Nourbese. *Showing Grit: Showboating North of the 44th Parallel*. Poui Publications, 1993.

———. *Frontiers: Essays on Writings on Racism and Culture*. Toronto: Mercury Press, 1992.

———. *Looking for Livingstone: An Odyssey of Silence*. Mercury Press, 1990.

———. *She Tries Her Tongue: Her Silence Softly Breaks*. Ragweed Press, 1989.

Poussaint, Alvin F. *Why Blacks Kill Other Blacks?* Emerson Hall, 1972.

Thomas, H Nigel. *Why We Write: Conversations with African Canadian Poets and Novelists*. TSAR Publications, 2006.

———. *From Folklore to Fiction: A Study of Folk Heroes and Rituals in the Black*

American Novel. Greenwood Press, 1988.
Walcott, Derek. "The Muse of History." In *Is Massa Day Dead?* Edited by Orde Coombs. Anchor Press/Doubleday: 1974.

"Beggaring the Nation"

Brooks, Peter. *Body Work: Objects of Desire in Modern Narrative*. Harvard UP, 1993.
Eustace, John. "Deregulating the Evacuated Body: Rohinton Mistry's 'Squatter.'" *Studies in Canadian Literature/Études en littérature canadienne* 28.1, 2003.
Foucault, Michel. *Discipline and Punish: The Birth of the Prison*. Penguin, 1991.
Gandhi, Mohandas K. "Brahmacharya." *Selected Writings of Mahatma Gandhi*, edited by Ronald Duncan. Beacon, 1951.
———. *Collected Works of Mahatma Gandhi*. Vol. 53. Government of India, 1977.
Grosz, Elizabeth. "Bodies-Cities." *Feminist Theory and the Body: A Reader*, edited by Janet Price and Margrit Shildrick. Routledge, 1999.
Kapur, Anuradha. "Intra-Culturalism and the Question of the Body." *Culture and the Making of Identity in Contemporary India*, edited by Kamala Ganesh and Usha Thakkar. Sage Publications, 2005.
Kristeva, Julia. *Powers of Horror: An Essay on Abjection*. Translated by Leon S Roudiez. Columbia UP, 1982.
Mills, James H. "Body as Target, Violence as Treatment: Psychiatric Regimes in Colonial and Postcolonial India." Mills and Sen, eds.
Mills, James H, and Satadru Sen, editors. *Confronting the Body: The Politics of Physicality in Colonial and Post-Colonial India*. Anthem, 2004.
Mistry, Rohinton. *A Fine Balance*. Random House, 1995.
Morey, Peter. "Post-Colonial DestiNations: Spatial Re(con)figurings in Khushwant Singh's *Train to Pakistan* and Rohinton Mistry's *A Fine Balance*." *Fictions of India: Narrative and Power*. Edinburgh UP, 2000.
———. *Rohinton Mistry*. Manchester UP, 2004.
———. "Terrible Beautification: Body Politics in Rohinton Mistry's *A Fine Balance*." *Angles on the English Speaking World* 1.1, 2001.
Tokaryk, Tyler. "Keynes, Storytelling, and Realism: Literary and Economic Discourse in Rohinton Mistry's *A Fine Balance*." *Studies in Canadian Literature/Études en littérature canadienne* 30.2, 2005.
Turner, Bryan S. "For the Sociology of the Body: An Analytical Review." *The Body: Social Process and Cultural Theory*, edited by Mike Featherstone, Mike Hepworth, and Bryan S Turner. Sage Publications, 2001.

Diasporic Violences, Uneasy Friendships, and Hiromi Goto's *The Kappa Child*

Bastien, Betty. *Blackfoot Ways of Knowing*. U of Calgary P, 2004.
Chandler, Graham. "Growing Their Own." *The Beaver*, February/March 2005.

Chow, Rey. "Against the Lures of Diaspora." In *Writing Diaspora*. Indiana UP, 1993.

Goto, Hiromi. *The Kappa Child*. Red Deer Press, 2001.

Laird, Gordon. "This Land Is Whose Land?" *This Magazine*, March-April 2000, www.thismagazine.ca/issues/2000/03/whoseland.php. Accessed 19 May 2008.

Miki, Roy. *Redress*. Raincoast, 2005.

Samsonite Corporation. "Vision and Heritage." corporate.samsonite.com/samsonite/about/vision_heritage/. Accessed 26 February 2008.

Austin Clarke's Poetic Turn

Algoo-Baksh, Stella. *Austin C Clarke: A Biography*. ECW Press, 1994.

Barrett, Paul. *Blackening Canada: Diaspora, Race, Multiculturalism*. U of Toronto, 2015.

Brand, Dionne. "An Ars Poetica from the Blue Clerk." Unpublished work.

Bucknor, Michael A. "'Voices Under the Window' of Representation: Austin Clarke's Poetics of (Body)-Memory in *The Meeting Point*." *Austin Clarke: Essays on His Works*, edited by Camille Isaacs. Guernica Editions, 2013.

Clarke, Austin. *The Bigger Light*. Little Brown, 1975.

———. "The Confessed Bewilderment of Martin Luther King and the Idea of Non Violence as a Political Tactic." *The Austin Clarke Reader*, edited by Barry Callaghan. Exile Editions, 1996.

———. *In Your Crib*. Guernica Editions, 2015.

———. *The Meeting Point*. Macmillan of Canada, 1967.

———. *More*. T Allen, 2008.

———. "The Motor Car." *When He Was Free and Young and He Used to Wear Silks*. Anansi, 1971.

———. *The Origin of Waves*. McClelland & Stewart, 1997.

———. *The Polished Hoe: A Novel*. T Allen, 2002.

———. *The Question*. M&S, 1999.

———. "Sometimes a Motherless Child". *The Austin Clarke Reader*, edited by Barry Callaghan. Exile Editions, 1996.

———. *Storm of Fortune*. Little, Brown, 1973.

———. *Where the Sun Shines Best*. Guernica Editions, 2013.

Quirt, Maggie. "'A Plea for Love and Blood': Social Justice in Austin Clarke's *Where the Sun Shines Best*." Edited by Camille Isaacs. *Austin Clarke: Essays on His Works*. Guernica Editions, 2013.

Thomas, H Nigel, editor. "Austin Clarke" in *Why We Write: Conversations with African Canadian Poets and Novelists: Interviews*. TSAR Publications, 2006.

Adrienne Rich. Quoted in Claudia Rankine, "Adrienne Riche's Poetic Transformations." *The New Yorker*. Web. 12 May 2016.

Sharpe, Christina. *In the Wake: On Blackness and Being*. Duke University Press, 2016.

Walcott, Derek. "The Saddhu of Couva". www.poemhunter.com/poem/the-saddhu-of-couva/. Accessed 16 July 2016.

Balancing in Silence: On Rienzi Crusz's Engagement with Myth

Bhaggiyadatta, Krisantha Sri. "English Wars." *Uddari Weblog.* 21 Sept. 2010. uddari.wordpress.com/2010/09/25/english-wars-by-krisantha-sri-bhaggiya-datta/ Accessed 28 March 2011.

Burnett, Paula. *Derek Walcott: Politics and Poetics.* UP Florida, 2000.

Crusz, Rienzi. *Beatitudes of Ice.* TSAR Publications, 1995.

———. *Flesh and Thorn.* Pasdeloup P, 1974.

———. *Elephant and Ice.* Porcupine's Quill, 1980.

———. *Enough To Be Mortal Now.* TSAR Publications, 2009.

———. *Insurgent Rain*, edited by Chelva Kanaganayakam. TSAR Publications, 1997.

———. *Singing Against the Wind.* Porcupine's Quill, 1985.

———. *Still Close to the Raven.* TSAR Publications, 1986.

———. *The Rain Doesn't Know Me Any More.* TSAR Publications, 1992.

Donne, John. *The Holy Sonnets.* Variorum Edition. Vol. 7. Part 1, edited by Gary Stringer. Indiana UP, 2005.

Frye, Northrop. *The Bush Garden: Essays in the Canadian Imagination.* Anansi, 1971.

Kanaganayakam, Chelva. *Dark Antonyms and Paradise.* TSAR Publications, 1997.

———. Introduction. *Insurgent Rain* by Rienzi Crusz, TSAR Publications, 1997.

Lincoln, Bruce. *Theorizing Myth: Narrative, Ideology and Scholarship.* U Chicago P, 1999.

Milton, John. *Paradise Lost.* W Wilson for John Bumpus, 1821.

Mukherjee, Arun. *Oppositional Aesthetics: Readings From A Hyphenated Space.* TSAR Publications, 1994.

Thorpe, Michael. Review. *The Rain Doesn't Know Me Any More* by Rienzi Crusz. *World Literature Today.* 68.1. 130-131. 1994.

Wikkramasinha, Lakdasa. "Don't Talk To Me About Matisse." *The Arnold Anthology of Post-colonial Literatures in English*, edited by J Thieme. Arnold P, 1996.

Postcolonial Mothering in Anita Rau Badami's *Tamarind Mem*

Badami, Anita Rau. *Tamarind Mem.* Vintage Canada, 2004.

Brown-Guillory, Elizabeth. *Women of Color: Mother-daughter Relationships in 20th-century Literature.* University of Texas Press, 1996.

Chodorov, Nancy. *The Reproduction of Mother: Psychoanalysis and the Sociology of Gender.* University of California Press, 1978.

Hirsch, Marianne. "Mothers and Daughters: A Review Essay." *Signs* 7.1, 1981.

———. *The Mother/Daughter Plot: Narrative, Psychoanalysis, Feminism.* Indiana UP, 1989.

Katrak, Ketu H. "Post-colonial Women's Colonized States: Mothering and m-othering in Bessie Head's A Question of Power and Kamala Das' My Story." *Journal of Gender Studies* 5.3, 1996.

McClintock, Anne. *Imperial Leather: Race, Gender and Sexuality in the Colonial*

Contest. Routledge, 1995.

Mohanram, Radhika. "The Problem of Reading: Mother-Daughter Relationships and Indian Postcoloniality, edited by Elizabeth Brown-Guillory. *Women of Color: Mother-Daughter Relationships in 20th Century Literature*. University of Texas Press, 1996.

O'Reilly, Andrea. "Across the Divide: Contemporary Anglo-American Feminist Theory on the Mother-Daughter Relationship." Edited by Sharon Abbey and Andrea O'Reilly. *Redefining Motherhood: Changing Identities and Patterns*. Second Story Press, 1998.

———. "Introduction." Andrea O'Reilly editor. *21st Century Motherhood: Experience, Identity, Policy, Agency*. Columbia UP, 2010.

Podnieks, Elizabeth and Andrea O'Reilly. "Introduction: Maternal Literatures in Text and Tradition, Daughter-Centric, Matrilineal, and Matrifocal Perspectives." Edited by Elizabeth Podnieks and Andrea O'Reilly. *Textual Mothers/Maternal Texts: Motherhood in Contemporary Women's Literatures*. Wilfred Laurier UP, 2010.

Rich, Adrienne. *Of Woman Born: Motherhood as Experience and Institution*. W W Norton, 1976.

Ruddick, Sara. *Maternal Thinking: Toward a Politics of Peace*. Beacon Press, 1989.

Sangha, Jasjit K. and Tahira Gonsalves. "Introduction" *South Asian Mothering: Negotiating Culture, Family and Selfhood*. Demeter Press, 2013.

Sayed, Asma. "Intersectional Interventions in Global Cinema: Introducing the Maternal." Edited by Asma Sayed. *Screening Motherhood in Contemporary World Cinema*. Demeter Press, 2016.

Trauma and Melancholia in H Nigel Thomas' *Behind the Face of Winter* and *No Safeguards*

Bartkowski, Frances. *Travelers Immigrants Inmates: Essays in Estrangement*. U of Minnesota P, 1995.

Buchwald, Emille, Pamela Fletcher, and Martha Roth, editors. *Transforming a Rape Culture*. Milkweed Editions, 1993

Conversations with Writers. www.conversationswithwriters.blogspot.com/2007/04/interview-with-h-nigel-thomas-author-of.html. Accessed 21 September 2016.

Du Bois, William E B. "Of Our Spiritual Thrivings." *The Souls of Black Folks*. Dover Publications, Inc., 1994.

Foster, Cecil. *a place called heaven The Meaning of Being Black in Canada*. Harper Perennial Canada, 1996.

———. Interview with Hubert Nigel Thomas. *Why We Write. Conversations with African Canadian Poets and Novelists*. Edited with and Introduction by H Nigel Thomas. Mawenzi House Publishers, 2006.

Goddard, Horace I. Review. *Moving Through Darkness* by H Nigel Thomas. *The Free Library*. 2002 Black Writers' Guild. Web. 10 August, 2016.

———. Confessions: A Review. *Behind the Face of Winter* by H Nigel Thomas. *The*

Free Library. 2002 Black Writers' Guild. Web. 10 August 2016.

———. "Thomas Opens the Book on Reading." *Montreal Community Contact*, 17 April 2015. www.montrealcommunitycontact.com/thomas-opens-the-book-on-reading. Accessed 20 September 2016.

Gokhale, Veena. "Courageous and Masterful Explorations of Otherness - An interview with H Nigel Thomas." www.montrealserai.com/2015/08/14/courageous-and-masterful-explorations-of-otherness-an-interview-with-h-nigel-thomas/. Accessed 28 September 2016.

Harris, Claire. *Drawing Down a Daughter*. Goose Lane Editions, 1992.

———. Interview with Hubert Nigel Thomas. *Why We Write. Conversations with African Canadian Poets and Novelists*. Edited with and Introduction by H Nigel Thomas. Mawenzi House Publishers, 2006.

Hodges, Hugh. Review. *Behind the Face of Winter* by H Nigel Thomas. *Quill & Quire*, Dec 2001, Vol. 67 Issue 12. www.connection.ebscohost.com/c/book-reviews/15857836/home-back-behind-face-winter. Accessed 25 September 2016.

Hoffmann, Alice. "H Nigel Thomas is on the verge of a breakthrough with *No Safeguards* Conversation with H Nigel Thomas." Web. Ian McGillis. 28 October 2015. www.montrealgazette.com/entertainment/books/h-nigel-thomas-is-on-the-verge-of-a-breakthrough-with-no-safeguards. Accessed 31 August 2016.

Hintzen, Percy C. *West Indians in the West: Self-Representation in an Immigrant Community*. New York UP, 2001.

Hutcheon, Linda and Marion Richmond. Introduction. *Other Solitudes: Canadian Multicultural Fictions*. Oxford UP, 1990.

Kaplan, Caren. *Questions of Travel: Postmodern Discourses of Displacement*. Duke UP, 1996.

Kasinitz, Philip, et al. "Fade to Black? The Children of West Indian Immigrants in Southern Florida." In *Ethnicities: Children of Immigrants in America*, edited by Rumbaut, RubJn G and Alejandro Portes. U of California P; Russell Sage Foundation, 2001.

Kuwabong, Dannabang. "Gatekeepers and gateways: Spiritualizing Gay masculinities in Nigel Thomas's *Spirits in the Dark*." *La Tore*. Año X, Núm. 36-37, 2005.

———. "Affirmative Melancholia or Paradox of Assimilation? Shifting Identities among African Caribbean-Canadians in H Nigel Thomas' *Behind the Face of Winter* and *Return to Arcadia*." Paper presented at the 36th Annual African Literature Association Conference, University of Arizona, Tucson, March 10-14, 2010.

Paquin, Éric. "Revue. De l'autre côté du miroir H Nigel Thomas, Des vies cassées, nouvelles, traduction de Lives. Whole and Otherwise par Alexie Doucet, Mémoire d'encrier." *Moebius: écritures/littérature*. Numéro 144, février 2015. http://id.erudit.org/iderudit/73454ac. Accessed 17 September 2016.

Pennebaker, James W. "Telling Stories: The Health Benefits of Narratives." *Literature and Medicine*. Vol. 19, 1, Spring.

Philip, Marlene Nourbese. *Harriet's Daughter*. Heinemann, 1988.

Stepick, Alex, et al. "Shifting Identities and Intergenerational Conflict: Growing up Haitian in Miami." In *Ethnicities: Children of Immigrants in America*, edited by Rumbaut, RubJn G and Alejandro Portes. U of California P, Russell sage Foundation, 2001.

Thomas, Hubert Nigel. *Behind the face of Winter*. Mawenzi House Publications, 2001.

———. *No Safeguards*. Guernica Editions, 2015.

———. *Return to Arcadia*. Mawenzi House Publications, 2007.

———. *Spirits in the Dark*. House of Anansi Press, 1987.

Walcott, Rinaldo. *Black Like Who? Writing Black Canada*. Insomnia Press, 1997.

Zhou, Min. "Straddling Different Worlds: The Acculturation of Vietnamese Refugee Children." In *Ethnicities: Children of Immigrants in America*, edited by Rumbaut, RubJn G and Alejandro Portes. U of California Press, Russell Sage Foundation, 2001.

Cyril Dabydeen's Amazing Corpus

Dabydeen, Cyril. *A Shapely Fire: Changing the Literary Landscape*. Mosaic Press, 1987.

———. *Another Way to Dance: Asian-Canadian Poetry*. Williams-Wallace Publications, 1998.

———. *Another Way to Dance: Contemporary Asian Poetry from Canada and the United States*. TSAR Publications, 1995.

———. *Berbice Crossing and Other Stories*. Peepal Tree Press Ltd., 1996.

———. *Black Jesus and other Stories*. TSAR Publications, 1996.

———. *Born in Amazonia*. Mosaic Press, 1995.

———. *Beyond Sangre Grande: Caribbean Writing Today*. TSAR Publications, 2011.

———. *Coastland: New and Selected Poems (1973-1989)*. Mosaic Press, 1989.

———. *Dark Swirl*. Peepal Tree Press Ltd., 1989.

———. *Discussing Columbus*. Peepal Tree Press Ltd., 1997.

———. *Distances*. Fiddlehead Poetry Books, 1977.

———. *Drums of my Flesh*. TSAR Publications, 2005.

———. *Elephants Make Good Stepladders*. Third Eye Publications, 1982.

———. *Goatsong*. Mosaic Press, 1977.

———. *Heart's Frame*. Vesta Publications, 1979.

———. *Imaginary Origins: Selected Poems (1970-2002)*. Peepal Tree Press Ltd., 2004.

———. *Islands Lovelier Than a Vision*. Peepal Tree Press Ltd., 1986.

———. *Jogging in Havana*. Mosaic Press, 1992.

———. *My Brahmin Days and Other Stories*. TSAR Publications, 2000.

———. *My Multi-Ethnic Friends and Other Stories*. Guernica Editions Inc., 2013.

———. *North of the Equator*. Beach Home Publishing, 2001.

———. *Play a Song Somebody: Selected Stories*. Mosaic Press, 2004.

———. *Poems in Recession*. Sadeek Press, 1972.

———. *Six Ottawa Poets*. Mosaic Press, 1990.
———. *Sometimes Hard*. Longmans, 1994.
———. *Still Close to the Island*. Commoners Press, 1980.
———. *Stoning the Wind*. TSAR Publications, 1994.
———. *This Planet Earth*. Borealis Press, 1979.
———. *To Monkey Jungle*. Third Eye, 1988.
———. *Wizard Swami*. 1985. Peepal Tree Press Ltd., 1988.

In Times of Upheaval: Cheran's Poetic Trajectory

Cheran, R. "Citizens of Many Worlds: Theorizing Tamil DiasporiCity." *History and Imagination: Tamil Culture in the Global Context*, edited by R Cheran, et al. TSAR Publications, 2007.
———. *Meendum Kadalukku*. Kalachuvadu, 2005.
———. *Nee Ippozhuthu Irangum Aaru*. Kalachuvadu, 2000.
———. Preface. *Maranathul Valvom*, edited by R Cheran et al. CreA, 1984.
Jeyamohan, B. *Kaalam*. December, 2008.
Kalachchuvadu, July-Sept. 99.
Ramaswamy, Sundara. *Kalachchuvadu*, 32, Nov-Dec, 2000.
Ravikumar, editor. *Waking is Another Dream*, Navayana, 2010.
Sivasegaram, S. *Vimarsanagal*. South Asian Books, 1995.
Sivathamby, K. *Tamil Elakkiath Thadam* 1980-2000. Moonravathu Manithan, 2000.
Walcott, Derek. *Selected Poetry*, Heinemann, 1993.

South Asian Poetry in Canada: In Search of a Place

Bannerji, Himani. "A Savage Aesthetic." Translated from Bengali. *A Separate Sky*. Domestic Bliss, 1982.
———. "Terror." *A Separate Sky*. Domestic Bliss, 1982.
Bhaggiyadatta, Krisantha Sri. "My Family." *Domestic Bliss*. Domestic Bliss, 1981.
Burke, Kenneth. *Permanence and Change: An Anatomy of Change* Bobbs-Merril, 1935.
Crusz, Rienzi. "The Sun-Man's Poetic Five Ways." *The Toronto South Asian Review* 1, 1, 1982.
Dabydeen, Cyril. "For the Sun Man." *Elephants Make Good Stepladders*. Third Eye, 1982.
———. "Lady Icarus." *Goatsong*. Mosaic Press, 1977.
———. "New Life." *This Planet Earth*. Borealis Press, 1979.
Davies, Ioan "Senses of Place," *Canadian Forum*, April 1982.
Gill, Lakshmi. "Song." *First Clearing (an immigrant's tour of life) poems*. Estaniel Press, 1972.
Hundal, Sukhwant. "A Letter to a Friend." Translated by Surjeet Kalsey. *Toronto South Asian Review* 2, 1, 1983.
Itwaru, Arnold. "Shattered Songs." *Nebula*, 1st Quarter, 1981.

Kalsey, Surjeet. "Siddhartha Does Penance Again." *Toronto South Asian Review* 2, 1, 1983.

Kroetsch, Robert, et al. *Canadian Ethnic Studies* 14, no 1, 1982.

Mukherji, Bharati. "An Invisible Woman," *Saturday Night*, March 1981.

Namjoshi, Suniti. "Philomel." *Feminist Fables*. Sheba Feminist Publishers, 1981.

———. "Poem Against Poets." *Shakti's Words: An Anthology of South Asian Canadian Women's Poetry*, edited by Diane McGifford and Judith Kearns. TSAR Publications, 1990.

Padmanab, S. "Night-Song." *Songs of the Slave* Vesta Publications, 1977.

Parameswaran, Uma. "Ganga Jal." Typescript received by this author from the poet. [—Editor's note: Subsequently published as "Chandrika" in *Shakti's Words*, edited by McGifford and Kearns, 1990]

———. untitled poem. *Toronto South Asian Review* l, 3, 1982.

Rao, Raja. "Foreword." *Kanthapura*. 2nd ed, Oxford University Press, 1974.

Rushdie, Salman. *Shame*. Rupa, 1983.

Weerasinghe, Asoka. "Sahelia." *Poems for Jeannie*. Vesta Publications, 1976.

Contributors

Frank Birbalsingh is Emeritus Professor and Senior Scholar of English at York University, Toronto. His publications include: *Frontiers of Caribbean Literature* (1996) and *Indian-Caribbean Test Cricketers and the Quest for Identity* (2016).

Aparna Halpé is Professor of English at Centennial College, Toronto. Her poetry has been published in various journals including *Channels*, the Journal of the English Writer's Cooperative, and *Postcolonial Text*. Her scholarly work has been published in *South Asian Diaspora* (Routledge), *Moving Worlds* (Leeds) and *Canadian Review of Comparative Literature* (UAlberta P). *Precarious* is Aparna's debut collection of poems.

James W Johnson is a graduate student in the Department of English at the University of Toronto. He has published papers in *Studies in Canadian Literature/ Études en littérature canadienne*, *Newfoundland and Labrador Studies*, and *The Journal of Student Writing*.

Chelva Kanaganayakam was Professor of English at Trinity College, University of Toronto. His major publications include *Moveable Margins: The Shifting Spaces of Canadian Literature* (2006), *Lutesong and Lament: Tamil Writing from Sri Lanka* (2001), *Dark Antonyms and Paradise: The Poetry of Rienzi Crusz* (1997), *Configurations of Exile: South Asian Writers and Their World* (1995), and *Structures of Negation: The Writings of Zulfikar Ghose* (1993).

Christine Kim is Associate Professor at Simon Fraser University. She is the author of *The Minor Intimacies of Race* (University of Illinois Press, 2016) and co-editor of *Cultural Grammars of Nation, Diaspora and Indigeneity* (Wilfrid Laurier UP,

2012). She has contributed chapters to essay collections on Asian Canadian literature and theatre, published articles in various journals, and is co-director of SFU's Institute of Transpacific Cultural Research.

DANNABANG KUWABONG teaches Caribbean literature at the University of Puerto Rico, San Juan. He has published three books: *Konga and other Dagaaba Folktales, Visions of Venom, Caribbean Blues & Love's Genealogy, Echoes from Dusty Rivers,* and *Voices from Kibuli Country.*

ARUN PRABHA MUKHERJEE is Professor of English at York University in Toronto. She is the author of *Postcolonialism: My Living* (1998), and *Oppositional Aesthetics* (1994), and numerous books and articles on postcolonial literatures, women's writing and critical theory. She is also the translator of *Joothan*, a novel by Omprakash Valmiki.

LESLIE SANDERS is University Professor in the Department of Humanities, York University. Her publications include *The Development of Black Theater in America*, two volumes of the performance works of Langston Hughes, and articles on Dionne Brand, Djanet Sears, Andrew Moodie, Austin Clarke.

ASMA SAYED is a scholar of Comparative Literature and Film Studies, whose interdisciplinary research focuses on Indian Ocean Studies, Postcolonial Literature, and South Asian diaspora in Canada. Her latest books include: *Screening Motherhood in Contemporary World Cinema* (2016), *M G Vassanji: Essays on His Work* (2014), and *Writing Diaspora: Transnational Memories, Identities and Cultures* (2014). She teaches English and Comparative Literature at MacEwan University.

H NIGEL THOMAS was a teacher with the Protestant School Board of Greater Montreal, before joining the faculty at Laval University, Quebec, from where he recently retired. His published works of fiction include *Behind the Face of Winter, Return to Arcadia, Lives, Whole and Otherwise* and *When the Bottom Falls Out.*